THE ACADEMIC WRITER'S TOOLKIT

To Yuko
my favorite
daughter-in-law

with love

Arthur Asa Berger

THE ACADEMIC WRITER'S TOOLKIT

A USER'S MANUAL

Arthur Asa Berger

Illustrated by the Author

Left Coast
Press Inc.

Walnut Creek, California

Left Coast Press Inc.

LEFT COAST PRESS, INC.
1630 North Main Street, #400
Walnut Creek, CA 94596
http://www.LCoastPress.com

ISBN 978-1-59874-138-4 hardcover
ISBN 978-1-59874-139-1 paperback

Library of Congress Cataloguing-in-Publication Data:

Berger, Arthur Asa, 1933–
   The academic writer's toolkit : a user's manual / Arthur Asa Berger.
     p. cm.
   Includes bibliographical references and index.
   ISBN 978-1-59874-138-4 (alk. paper) —
   ISBN 978-1-59874-139-1 (pbk. : alk. paper)
   1. English language—Rhetoric—Handbooks, manuals, etc. 2. Report writing—
Handbooks, manuals, etc. 3. Academic writing—Handbooks, manuals, etc. I. Title.
PE1408.B477 2008
808'.042—dc22   2008014015

Printed in the United States of America

08 09 10 11 12 5 4 3 2 1

Contents

PART II: GENRES OF ACADEMIC WRITING

Acknowledgments

I want to thank Mitch Allen, the editor of Left Coast Press, Inc., for suggesting I write this book and three others that I'm working on. Over the past twenty-five years, I've written many books for Mitch, and it has always been quite an experience—especially delightful since I love to revise and rewrite my book manuscripts four or five times. Mitch is adventurous (some might say foolhardy) and has published some of my academic murder mysteries, which I really appreciate. As a matter of fact, he has asked me to write a new one on material culture.

I owe my gratitude to Brenda Hadenfeldt, my editor when she worked at Rowman & Littlefield, for her help with this book. She offered suggestions and invaluable advice about every part of every chapter of this book. In the course of my education, I took courses in creative writing with the marvelous Marguerite Young at the University of Iowa and the distinguished poet and novelist Allen Tate at the University of Minnesota, and I believe I gained a great deal from those courses and from having the opportunity to spend time with these writers. I also want to thank all the remarkably talented copyeditors who have been so instrumental in helping me avoid errors of one kind or another and in polishing my writing.

Finally, I'd like to express my appreciation to all those authors who have written books on writing (in general), academic writing, research, and related concerns from which I've quoted material. I've cited their names in the bibliography.

Introduction
Mission Impossible?

I spend my days among academics in the humanities, a vast majority of whom make a profession of being pretentious. Writing, for them, is about obfuscation: Rather than enlightening a discussion, they make it more obscure. The state of literary criticism among them is even more dismal: It is self-obsessed, self-contained, and self-referential, hiding behind terminologies that only a small group of initiated readers are able to grasp. But not much happens when they do. That is because this type of reflection is utterly useless.

—Illan Stavans, "Wilson Critiqued Literature
When Books Really Mattered," M3.

Man possesses the ability to construct languages capable of expressing every sense, without having any idea how each word has meaning or what its meaning is—just as people speak without knowing how the individual sounds are produced.

Everyday language is part of the human organism and is no less complicated than it. It is not humanly possible to gather immediately from it what the logic of language is.

Language disguises thought. So much so, that from the outward form of the clothing it is impossible to infer the form of the thought beneath it, because the outward form of the clothing is not designed to reveal the form of the body, but for entirely different purposes.

The tacit conventions on which the understanding of everyday language depends are enormously complicated.

—Ludwig Wittgenstein, "Understanding Depends on
Tacit Conventions," 35–37.

1

The room was empty, except for a small table on which rested a small tape recorder and a large manila envelope. I walked to the table and pressed the button on the tape recorder. A voice started speaking. I recognized the voice. It was M:

> Good morning, Arthur. Your mission, should you wish to accept it, is to write a book on academic writing for professors and future professors. It should give them various tools that will help them improve the kind of writing that is often required in academic institutions. At the same time, it should be interesting and highly readable. In the event that you are captured by composition theorists or by linguistics professors, we cannot rescue you. Photographs of the members of your team who can help you will be found in the envelope. This tape will self-destruct in three seconds.

Three seconds after the message ended, there was a loud hiss and the tape burned up. I opened the envelope and took out the photographs—Roland Barthes, Aristotle, M. M. Bakhtin, Jan Morris, Ludwig Wittgenstein, Conrad Hyers, Aaron Wildavsky, E. B. White, William Strunk, Lev Vygotsky, Roman Jakobson, Sigmund Freud, William Zinsser, Raymond Queneau, and a number of others. I left the room and drove home. I went into my house, headed straight for my study, sat down at my desk, and started tearing up pieces of paper.

Not an Impossible Task

The Academic Writer's Toolkit is organized in two parts. In part I, I deal with such topics as making your writing more readable, developing a personal style, and using aids such as diagrams and charts to make your material easier to understand. I also share my ideas about outlining and using a journal creatively, as well as offer some general "rules" for writing.

In part II, I present genres—documents that academics are often called upon to write, including memos, letters, reports, research articles, and books. I offer many suggestions—the "tools" in our kit—to help you write your texts in a more readable and interesting style.

I assume, of course, you are already a competent writer. This book helps you become a *better* writer. Think of me as a coach. In some cases, I stress fundamentals. In other cases, I offer suggestions that provide new insights about writing. Just about every professional athlete has a coach. So why shouldn't professors, who are often called upon to do a good deal of writing, have writing coaches?

I was assigned this "impossible task" because I've written more than a hundred articles for newspapers and scholarly journals in the United States and abroad. In addition, I've written more than sixty books, many of which have been translated into foreign languages. I also have taught writing for more than thirty years. Some people argue that while you can teach grammar, you can't teach writing. They believe that writers have to learn "the hard way" what works and what doesn't and must figure out, on their own, how to develop a personal style. "You may be able to help writers with certain fundamentals such as grammar and punctuation and ways of organizing papers," they say, "but you can't teach writing."

I disagree.

There are, to be sure, many people who don't have "a way with words" and who find writing painful. I would suggest that this is because they've never been taught how to write, how to organize their time, how to outline, or discipline their writing. This is where having a coach can help. After reading this book you may not end up as a masterful stylist like Jan Morris, whose work I'll be discussing shortly, but you'll know more about how to write more stylishly, how to plan and write academic texts of all kinds, and how to function more effectively as a writer. And you'll probably have a better idea about the steps involved in publishing a book. There's more to it than having lunch with editors.

The Academic Writer's Toolkit is, in the final analysis, a book about expository writing, the most common kind of writing in academic settings. But the insights offered here can be used in other forms of writing as well. This book is a personal one, written in an informal manner and discursive in nature, because that is my style of writing and the style that I think is best suited to my ideas. I hope my book will help you to develop your own writing style and that you will be able to use the insights you gain from this book to best express your ideas in a clear and readable manner, different from the kind of writing Illan Stavans described in the epigraph above.

On the Power of Language: Jan Morris on India

If you want to get an idea about the power of words to affect our ideas and generate an emotional response, I offer this quotation from a brilliant stylist, the travel writer Jan Morris. Her description of India, taken from her book

Destinations: Essays from Rolling Stone, is simply remarkable. This essay, "Delhi," was written in 1975, so her statistics about the population of India are no longer correct—they are off by 500 million people, give or take 100 million—but everything else is right on the mark. She writes:

> Of all the world's countries, India is the most truly prodigious, and this quality of astonishment displays itself afresh every day as the sun comes up in Delhi. Five-hundred-and-eighty-million people, three-hundred languages, provinces from the Himalayan to the equatorial, cities as vast as Bombay and Calcutta, villages so lost in time that no map marks them, nuclear scientists and aboriginal hillmen, industrialists of incalculable wealth and dying beggars sprawled on railway platforms, three or four great cultures, myriad religions, pilgrims from across the world, politicians sunk in graft, the Grand Trunk Road marching to Peshawar, the temples of Madras gleaming in the sun, an inexhaustible history, an incomprehensible social system, an unfathomable repository of human resource, misery, ambiguity, vitality and confusion—all this, the colossal corpus of India, invests, sprawls around, infuses, elevates, inspires and very nearly overwhelms New Delhi. (45)

The second sentence is 112 words long and piles fact upon fact and superlative upon superlative to give readers a sense of the awesome and incredible nature of life in India.

Jan Morris uses language in a way calculated to astound her readers. She starts with an assessment of India. It is *truly prodigious.* Putting the "truly" in this sentence makes her argument stronger, and "punches" the term "prodigious." Then she offers some amazing statistics and moves on to extraordinary details about India: vast cities and nameless towns, nuclear scientists and aboriginal hillmen, incalculably wealthy industrialists, and dying beggars.

These are not simple oppositions but extreme ones, and they project a country that is, in nearly every way, almost beyond belief. Morris moves on to using adjectives and here, too, she deals with extremes: India's history is *inexhaustible,* her social system *incomprehensible,* her human resources *unfathomable,* and the corpus of India *colossal.* She concludes this passage with powerful verbs: India, she writes, inspires, invests, infuses, and *overwhelms.* (*Italics mine.*)

Travel writing is different from the kind of writing you will be called upon to do, and you won't have the latitude Jan Morris had, as a travel writer, to play with language the way she did. But from reading this passage you can get a sense of the power words have to shape ideas, impressions, and emotions. After reading this passage, my image of India was deeply affected. You should do whatever you can to make sure that your writing, whatever kind it is, has as much vitality and presence as possible, without violating the canons of good taste or propriety.

Learning from Narratives

I tell some stories in this book. Stories, or narratives, are important modes of learning. As Laurel Richardson states in her article, "Narrative and Sociology":

> Narrative is the primary way through which humans organize their experiences into temporally meaningful episodes. . . . Narrative is both a mode of reasoning *and* a mode of representation. People can "apprehend" the world narratively and people can "tell" about the world narratively. According to Jerome Bruner . . . narrative reasoning is one of the two basic and universal human cognition modes. The other mode is the logico-scientific . . . the logico-scientific mode looks for universal truth conditions, whereas the narrative mode looks for particular connections between events. Explanation in the narrative mode is contextually embedded, whereas the logico-scientific explanation is extracted from spatial and temporal events. Both modes are "rational" ways of making meaning. (118)

I have included some narratives in this book—not only to teach elements of academic writing, but also to avoid the dry-as-dust style often found in textbooks and other academic books.

The Importance of Humor: A Zen Writing Book

When I taught, my students often claimed they didn't know how to understand me—they never knew when I was serious and when I was putting them on. I would describe my teaching method as follows: "I fool around, and one way or another—somehow—my students learn." In my courses, I often devised learning games and lectured in a discursive, elliptical, and humorous way.

I've adopted that style in this book, using humor as well as narratives to further my goal—to help you learn how to write with more style and in a more readable manner. My whimsical style doesn't mean my writing isn't academic in nature. I would caution, however, that if you are a faculty member at a university, it's best to adopt this style only when you are a full professor; alas, some professors and academic administrators are put off by anything personal, amusing, or entertaining. As we'll see in later chapters, there are tricks to using humor effectively, and some genres lend themselves better to this approach than others. But humor in writing gets your readers' attention and serves as a useful teaching tool.

Zen masters also taught by joking and clowning around, so you can think of this book as being "zen" in nature. When the Zen masters asked, "What is the sound of one hand clapping?" they were using games to teach important lessons about life. As Conrad Hyers writes in *Zen and the Comic Spirit*:

> A glance at some of the common features of comic lines, behavior or situations reveals a close analogy between comic techniques and Zen techniques; as well as the serviceability of comic techniques in Zen: irrationality, contradiction, incongruity, absurdity, irrelevancy, triviality, nonsense, distortion, abruptness, shock, sudden twist, reversal or overturning. In both comedy and Zen one is prevented from drawing a purely intellectual conclusion at the end of an argument and therefore entering the abstractness and deceptiveness of a pseudo-appropriation of truth. (142)

My writing style also uses humor for didactic purposes, but I won't torture you with puzzling Zen statements such as "What is the difference between a crocodile? (The answer: it swims in water and not on land!)?" Instead, let me share an experience that taught me, with much humor, a valuable lesson about a writer's intentions and a reader's interpretations.

Has Everything I've Written Really Been Fiction?

In the summer of 2000, I gave lectures in Vietnam at several institutions of higher education. During one lecture, I read from a book I wrote about American everyday life, called *Bloom's Morning*, originally entitled *Ulysses Sociologica*. My idea in writing the book was to do for sociology and cultural anthropology what James Joyce did for literature. I would take one day in the life of a typical American and analyze the various objects he used and rituals he observed. He, like the hero of Joyce's novel, was named Bloom. I soon realized that writing about an entire day was too massive for one book so I concentrated on Bloom's morning.

In *Bloom's Morning* I analyze and interpret such objects as broadloom rugs, bathrobes, electric toothbrushes, toasters, and trash compactors, and such rituals as taking showers, putting on stockings, shaving, making toast, and reading the morning newspaper. These short essays, thirty-five in all, are sandwiched between a lengthy theoretical discussion of everyday life and a concluding section discussing cultural analysis.

After I had read aloud from several short chapters—on my interpretations of toasters, trash compactors, and gel toothpaste—one of the Vietnamese professors at my lecture asked me an interesting question:

"Is *Bloom's Morning* a novel?"

I was both startled and amused by this question. I had thought of my book as a somewhat whimsical semiotic, sociological, and psychoanalytic decoding and interpreting of American everyday life and culture, but here was someone asking me whether what I had written was, in reality, a work of fiction.

What follows is one of my favorite passages in *Bloom's Morning*—on toasters and toast. It will give you an idea of what the thirty-five middle chapters are like. You can decide for yourself whether the professor's question was a legitimate one.

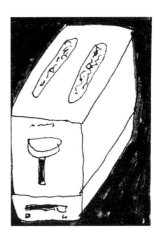

An interesting philosophical problem is raised by the toaster. What is toast—the product of a process or the process itself? That is, does bread become toast (and change its identity somehow) or do we toast bread and thereby only modify its character slightly? Is toast bread that has been processed (toasted) or changed (made into toast)? Obviously we start off with a piece of bread—and for our purposes, let us assume that we have the standard loaf of sliced pan bread with its thin crust. The question is whether we end up with a variation of the piece of sliced bread or something that is different. In terms of the dynamics of American culture, I would suggest that we would like to think that toast is something different from bread, per se. That is, the process involves a major transformation (in the same way that grinding a steak turns it into hamburger). We believe in the power of change and in our ability to change our circumstance and status. (157)

Later it dawned on me that this Vietnamese professor might not be the only one to consider my books as works of fiction.

Granted, I have written and published a number of academic mystery novels. These mysteries deal with the violent (though fictional) murder of professors and, at the same time, investigate some subject such as postmodernism or sociological theory or literary criticism. I love to fictionally bump off professors, and so far I've killed around twenty of them, in a number of different ways, in my books. In my bloodiest mystery, *The Hamlet Case*, I kill six professors—but not before each offers a different interpretation of *Hamlet*. These novels have often been successful as course texts. Four have been translated into

Chinese. My first one, *Postmortem for a Postmodernist,* has been used in cultural theory classes and has been reprinted a number of times. But in each of these cases, I wrote a novel intending for it to be a novel. Could it be that my various nonfiction professional books and textbooks, which I assumed were academic or scholarly, were actually novels without my knowing it?

What I learned from my experience in Vietnam was that you never can tell how what you've written will be interpreted, even though you are fairly confident that others won't misunderstand or misinterpret your work. Of course I was only reading from a couple of chapters of *Bloom's Morning,* and things like trash compactors—the subject of one of the chapters I read to my audience in Vietnam—are quite foreign to people there. Nevertheless, the story points to the need to get your message across clearly, even if it involves making summaries and repeating yourself to do so.

Writing Myself into Existence

In most of the books I've written, the section about the author comes at the very end of the book, hidden away there by the editors. But since this is a very personal book, I'd like to say something about myself right away—so you'll understand more about my ideas about writing.

When I was in high school, I knew that I wanted some kind of a "creative" career but didn't know whether I should be an artist or a writer. So I consulted numerous career counselors. After giving me various preference tests, every one of these counselors suggested that I pursue a career in advertising. As it turns out, I've spent much of the past forty years writing about many of the negative aspects of advertising and its corrosive effects on American consumer culture.

At the time, I found myself drawn to the written word, so I became a writer. Originally I thought I'd be a journalist, and after earning my bachelor's degree in literature and philosophy at the University of Massachusetts–Amherst, I enrolled at the University of Iowa for an master's in journalism. I also took advantage of the renowned Writers' Workshop there and studied with a remarkable woman, the writer and novelist Marguerite Young. She worked for nineteen years on a 1,200-page novel, *Miss MacIntosh My Darling.* She taught me the importance of using my imagination when I wrote and of not being constrained by fears of how others might receive my writings.

It was in 1954 in Iowa City, the "Athens of the Midwest," that I started keeping a journal. Since then I've completed eighty-five journals, each of more than two hundred pages, as well as other, smaller journals I keep when traveling. All of my books, including this one, originated from my notes in these journals. They are full of charts and diagrams and pages devoted to brainstorming. In between the creative sections, I complain about colleagues, academic administrators, editors, and the weather. I write about what I'm *going* to write and then, after working at the computer, I write about what I've written.

Some pages from my journals, showing my brainstorming and list-making are reproduced in chapter 2, where I will say more about using journals as a writing tool. Keeping a journal is a wonderful way to "warm up" for any writing you might do. And, at the end of your career, you may have eighty-five volumes of notes to work from when you come to write your memoir.

Through my journal writing, I've had the feeling that, in some way, I've written myself into existence. Keeping journals reminds me of things I've done, places I've gone, and ideas I've had. Our memories may fade, but the written word lives on. In my journals I have a record of what I was doing, what I was thinking, and, when I was traveling, where I was and what experiences I had, for just about every day for the past fifty years.

The English philosopher George Berkeley, for whom the University of California, Berkeley, is named, once wrote "to be is to be perceived." I would amend that and suggest "to write is to be perceived by your readers and the way you write shapes the way you are perceived." Not only did I write myself into existence in my journals, I also became a writer by writing in my journals, for it is in them that I have developed my style and worked on my ideas, played around with concepts, and figured out how to add humorous touches to my writing to make it more lively.

This chapter offers you a glimpse of my notions on writing and the way tools such as keeping a journal can help a writer both develop as a stylist and become a more creative and imaginative thinker. This *Toolkit* is designed to help you become more aware of the need to develop a distinctive style and become more tuned in to the audiences for which you are writing. When you've finished this book I think you'll agree that writing in an interesting and informative style is not "mission impossible."

PART I

THE WRITING PROCESS

The Academic Writer's Toolkit

In the broadest sense all writing is about yourself. Even your laundry list. Wise readers have always known that words reveal the person. Every kind of prose—exposition, argument, description—tells us something about the writer.

—Thomas S. Kane and Leonard J. Peters, *Writing Prose*, 3

Words that convey no information may nevertheless move carloads of shaving cream or cake mix, as we all know from television commercials. Words can start people marching in the streets—and can stir others to stoning the marchers. Words that make no sense as prose can make a great deal of sense as poetry. Words that seem simple and clear to some may be puzzling and obscure to others. With words we sugarcoat our nastiest motives and our worst behavior, but with words we also formulate our highest ideals and aspirations. (Do the words we utter arise as a result of our thoughts, or are our thoughts determined by the linguistic systems we happen to have been taught?) To understand how language works, what pitfalls it conceals, what its possibilities are, is to understand what is central to the complicated business of living the life of a human being.

—S.I. Hayakawa, *Language in Thought and Action,* vii

Literally speaking, tools are tangible devices that we use to make or do things. But a broader definition of tools includes anything we use to accomplish a task. In *Academic Writer's Toolkit*, our tools are strategies and suggestions to aid in the process of writing. Before choosing specific tools, let's begin with a look at the term "academic" and at academic writing, in general.

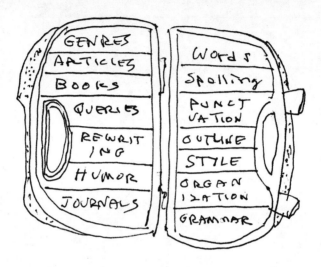

Defining Academic Writing

There are a number of definitions of the term "academic" in popular culture, most of them negative. Dictionary definitions, for the most part, tie the term to scholarship and university settings. One stereotype suggests that academics are so deeply involved in their research and other scholarly pursuits that they are often unaware of what is going on in the "real world," the world outside the academy. These academics are generally viewed as incapable of functioning in this real world.

Another stereotype suggests that academics focus on theoretical concerns without any regard for practical matters. These stereotypes include absent-minded professors—often viewed as inept, boring, even ridiculous. The term "academic" functions as a framing device for all the negative attitudes listed above. This frame also affects our perceptions about what we will find when we read academic writing, but there's no reason why academic writing can't be as interesting and vibrant as that of the best travel writers and others who write for the general public.

I understand academic writing to mean *expository writing, generally done in university settings, that observes certain rules and conventions about what is appropriate as far as the content and style of what is written are concerned.* In the passage that follows, by Thomas S. Kane and Leonard J. Peters from *Writing Prose*, we find a more comprehensive discussion of exposition:

> Different kinds of writing achieve different purposes. On the basis of controlling purpose, we traditionally divide all prose into three kinds: narration, description, and exposition. Of these, exposition is especially important to the college student since much of what he reads, and most of what he writes, is expository prose. Exposition is writing that explains. In generally, it answers the questions how? And why? If we go into any university library, most of the books we find on the shelves are examples of exposition. (169)

There are many different kinds of academic writing—from book reviews and scholarly essays to monographs, theses, doctoral dissertations, and books. But just because a written text is academic doesn't mean it must be boring or filled with jargon. You can offer your readers answers to the "why" and "how" questions that Kane and Peters mention in a readable and accessible style—and should work hard to do so.

Some academic writers adopt a style full of hypersyllabic Latinate words and jargon with a purpose in mind. These writers are concerned with technical matters or complicated concepts and are writing for specialized audiences of other academics familiar with the jargon used. In such cases, the use of this kind of writing is understandable.

Philosophers, for example, are notorious for writing in a convoluted style that is often unintelligible and impenetrable to anyone except other philosophers. Consider the following passage from Immanuel Kant's masterwork, *Groundwork of the Metaphysics of Morals*:

> Since the universality of the law governing the production of effects constitutes what is properly called *nature* in its most general sense (nature as regards form)—that is, the existence of things so far as determined by universal laws—the universal imperative of duty may also run as follows: *"Act as if the maxim of your action were to become through your will a universal law of nature."*

This extremely complicated sentence, sixty-eight words long, expresses one of Kant's most important and influential ideas: the existence of a "categorical imperative." This idea, of acting as if our actions were to become universal has been, it turns out, one of the most fundamental concepts in Western ethics. But because of the complex nature of Kant's ideas and the complicated sentence structure found in this passage, the writing is difficult to read and understand.

Not all philosophers write this way. Depending on the purpose of the writing and the audience addressed, even philosophers can be informal, conversational, or irreverent. Consider, for example, this course description written by the philosopher Robert Nozick in the Harvard University bulletin:

> *Philosophy 25: The Best Things in Life*
> A philosophical examination of the nature and value of those things deemed best, such as friendship, love, intellectual understanding, sensual pleasure, achievement, adventure, play, luxury, fame, power, enlightenment, and ice cream.

He lists some of the "best" topics included in his course and ends his description with a playful and comedic touch—ice cream. Since professors need to "sell" their courses, they sometimes write course descriptions that will attract students.

Woody Allen has seized upon the college bulletin course description genre and written a wonderful parody of the typical course description in "Spring Bulletin," which appeared in the *New Yorker* in 1967 and was later published in *Getting Even*:

> *Philosophy 1:* Everyone from Plato to Camus is read and the following topics are covered: Ethics: The categorical imperative and six ways to make it work for you. Aesthetics: Is art the mirror of life, or what? Metaphysics: What happens to the soul after death? How does it manage? Epistemology: Is knowledge knowable? If not, how do we know this? The Absurd: Why existence is often considered silly, particularly for men who wear brown and white shoes. Manyness and oneness are studies as they relate to otherness. (Students achieving oneness will move ahead to twoness.) (44)

Woody Allen's description is intended as humor, of course, and obviously if you're writing for other professors and are addressing difficult and complex issues, you write differently than if you're writing to persuade college sophomores to take a course. I'll discuss audiences later in this chapter; first, let's take a moment to read two examples of academic prose, written by the same person but for different audiences.

Two Examples of Academic Writing

Typical examples of pedantic academic writing are often found in scholarly books and specialized journals. This writing generally has a high level of abstraction and makes use of technical language with which the readers are familiar. For example, the following selection is from Todd Gitlin's "Television Screens: Hegemony in Transition," which appeared in *Media and Mass Culture*, a book edited by David Lazare:

> These tensions within hegemonic ideology render it vulnerable to the demands of insurgent groups and to cultural change in general. Insurgencies press upon the hegemonic whole in the name of one of its components—against the demands of others. *And popular culture is one crucial institution where the rival claims of ideology are sometimes pressed forward, sometimes reconciled in imaginative form.* Popular culture absorbs oppositional ideology, adapts it to the contours of the core hegemonic principle, and domesticates it. (*Emphasis in original.*) (242)

If readers don't know what "hegemony" and "ideology" mean, it will be hard for them to figure out what Gitlin, a sociologist at Columbia University, is writing about. But since this passage is from a chapter in an academic anthology on media, readers most likely are familiar with these concepts.

Gitlin often writes in a more accessible style. For example, in *Media Unlimited*, his discussion of news is very readable:

> The news is not in any simple way a "mirror" on the world; it is a conduit for ideas and symbols, an industrial product that promotes packages of ideas and ideologies, and serves, consequently, as social ballast, though at times also a harbinger of social change. The news is a cognitive wrap. The world is this way; the media make it appear that way. (2)

As this passage demonstrates, academic writing doesn't have to be dull, boring, turgid, and riddled with jargon. In this passage, Gitlin quite obviously was writing for a different and more general audience; he thus adopted a different style.

What Communication Theory Can Teach Us about Writing

Whether you are writing stand-up comedy, minutes from a department meeting, or a jargon-ladened poststructuralist cultural analysis, it is useful to understand what it means to "communicate." As a recently retired professor of communication, I'd like to offer you a brief introduction to communication theory so you can better understand the process of communication when you write.

There are many theories that attempt to explain the process of communication. I won't enumerate them here. The one I have found most useful—and one of the most widely cited—is that of Roman Jakobson, a famous linguistics scholar. In his essay "Linguistics and Poetics" (quoted in ed. David Lodge, *Modern Criticism and Theory*), he writes:

> Language must be investigated in all the variety of its functions. . . . An outline of these functions demands a concise survey of the constitutive factors in any speech event, in any act of verbal communication. The ADDRESSER sends a MESSAGE to the ADDRESSEE. To be operative the message requires a CONTEXT referred to ("referent" in another, somewhat ambiguous nomenclature), seizable by the addressee, and either verbal or capable of being verbalized; a CODE fully, or at least partially, common to the addresser and addressee (or in other words, to the encoder and decoder of the message); and finally, a CONTACT, a physical channel and psychological connection between the addresser and addressee, enabling both of them to enter and stay in communication. All these factors inalienably involved in verbal communication may be schematized as follows:

| | CONTEXT | |
| ADDRESSER | MESSAGE | ADDRESSEE |

CONTACT
CODE

(34)

Jakobson's diagram shows the relation among the various factors in communication. Let me use Jakobson's theory to explain written communication. The most important elements of this theory are as follows:

- a **writer** (addresser) who sends
- a **message** (the content of a written text) to
- a **reader** (addressee, usually a professor or an editor) using
- a **code** (the language used) and
- a **contact** (for our purposes, the text itself that is passed in).

In Jakobson's terms, I am the addresser (or writer) who sends a number of messages (about academic writing) to addressees (readers like you) using the code of English in a contact/text (this book). If my style of writing is suitable and the material I send is useful, there is reason to hope I'll find a decent number of addressees for my *Toolkit*. When you write something, you always hope that what you write will be of interest and use to others—that your message is valuable to your readers and uses an understandable and engaging code.

Writers should keep in mind these basic elements in communication. The way we do this is what I would describe as "style." In the section that follows, I will be discussing your need to think about the audiences for your writing, what Jakobson called your "addressees," and later in the book I will deal with ways of finding appropriate language for your readers and other matters related to Jakobson's theory.

On Audience

In the advertising world, copywriters and creative directors focus on what they call the "target audience"—the primary audience for their message. Advertisers work hard to make sure that their material is suited to their target audience and, with luck, to other audiences. You should do the same by focusing your attention on a target audience.

This means that the style of writing you adopt should be suited to your readers. If you are a professor in an academic institution, and you submit an article to a journal, your article will likely be evaluated by a group of professors, who function as editors and gatekeepers to determine whether the readers of the journal—your target audience—will read what you have written. You will be expected to write, generally speaking, in a formal (and not a loose and conversational) style, to have a coherent logical organization to your work, and to offer evidence you've gathered in your research as well as, in some cases, from experts and authorities to support your thesis or contentions. You should avoid jargon and an obscure writing style to the extent this is possible.

In their classic work, *The Elements of Style*, William Strunk Jr. and E.B. White discuss the relationship between style and the writer's sense of self as it relates to audiences:

> If one is to write, one must believe—in the truth and worth of the scrawl—in the ability of the reader to receive and decode the message. No one can write decently who is distrustful of the reader's intelligence, or whose attitude is patronizing. (77)

That is, you must respect your target audience and find a way to satisfy its needs, as you see them, and also satisfy yourself, the subject of my next discussion.

Writing for Readers and Yourself

Writing for yourself means writing in a way that pleases you and that you hope will please others. To do this, strike a balance between what you would write if your intended audience were of little concern and what you would write if your only purpose was to reach a specific audience. You must keep in mind literary conventions, the requirements of your potential publishers, the nature of the genre you are writing in, and the needs and desires of your intended audience. Writing is always an act of faith and is based on confidence—that what you have to say will find an audience who will respond to your writing the way you want them to and a publisher who will take a chance on publishing what you've written.

A good deal depends on what you are writing. Obviously, writing a memo isn't as challenging as writing a scholarly article or a report; you also won't get the same kind of feeling of accomplishment for memos, e-mail messages, and other kinds of everyday writing that you get from writing a dissertation or a book. But regardless of what kind of writing you are doing, you should always feel good about what you have written, since everything you write is a representation of your intellect and your personality.

Talk Is Cheap

When I was in graduate school in the early 1960s, I taught Freshman English. I shared an office with three other graduate students, two of whom decided to write an article together. They spent years talking about the piece they planned to write. As far as I know, they never wrote it.

It's easy to talk endlessly about articles and books you plan to write. The hard part is actually writing them. Writing takes real work. Universities are full of corridor chatterers and conceptualists, who talk day and night about the research they are going to do and the great works they are going to write, but who never get around to doing the research or actually writing anything. Don't get caught in this trap. The important thing is to get something down on paper as soon as possible.

I once had an academic colleague who prided himself on his ability to criticize other works. He took great pleasure in tearing apart articles and books, revealing what he thought to be their inadequacies. He once told me that all of my books—I had a dozen at the time—

were "unpublishable," and that I had only succeeded in getting them published because I tricked gullible editors into accepting them.

I couldn't help but laugh.

When I asked him why he had never published anything, he replied, "My work is too good to be published." And that's where I let things stand between us. I continued to publish my "unpublishable" articles and books, while he published nothing because his work was "too good" for that. He continued terrorizing his students with his mean-spirited criticism of their essays and term papers. People like him, I believe, have made many young students afraid of writing term papers and other kinds of academic writing. I would imagine that he never wrote anything because of his own fears—because he was afraid that if he did, he'd be subjecting his ideas (and his ego) to the scrutiny of others.

There's no need to be afraid of writing. In the later chapters of this book I will offer practical advice on style and process, including how to foil writer's block and keep the words flowing. I will describe a method of outlining that I use in plotting out my books. I will also discuss the use of transitions in writing, different styles writers can adopt to suit their needs, various forms or genres of academic writing, and what is involved in publishing one's writings.

All of the tools that I am offering are based on what I've learned during the course of forty years of teaching writing and of writing hundreds of book reviews, articles, scholarly books, and textbooks. My suggestions are not rigid rules to obey—although obeying standard rules of grammar is generally good practice. Writing is a form of creative activity. All writers, including you, have different approaches to their craft, based on their personalities, the kind of project, and the audiences they wish to address. But first of all, you must begin by writing.

The Writing Process
Ideas and Research

Writing for the Stage: All drama is conflict. Character development is also very important. Also, what they say. Students learn that long, dull speeches are not so effective, while short "funny" ones seem to go over well. Simplified audience psychology is explored: Why is a play about a lovable old character named Gramps often not as interesting in the theatre as staring at the back of someone's head and trying to make him turn around?

—Woody Allen, "Spring Bulletin," 46

Idea for story: Some beavers take over Carnegie Hall and perform *Wozzek*. (Strong theme. What will be the structure?)

Short story: A man awakens in the morning and finds himself transformed into his own arch supports. (This idea can work on many levels. Psychologically, it is the quintessence of Kruger, Freud's disciple, who discovered sexuality in bacon.)

Play idea: a character based on my father, but without quite so prominent a big toe. He is sent to the Sorbonne to study the harmonica. In the end, he dies, never realizing his one dream—to sit up to his waist in gravy. (I see a brilliant second-act curtain, where two midgets come upon a severed head in a shipment of volleyballs.)

—Woody Allen, "Selections from the Allen Notebooks"

In the passages just quoted, Woody Allen ponders, tongue in cheek, many wild and wonderful ideas for plays and stories. He pokes fun at some of the crazy stuff done by avant garde artists and theoreticians of all kinds. Allen has a distinctive voice—one that makes it possible for many people to recognize his stories by their absurdity, as well as by his use of language and style of writing. Allen also writes with confidence—a sense of security about his mastery of plot, language, and comic timing—that readers can easily sense in his short stories and other works.

Allen's ability to play with ideas, in a humorous vein, is an example of how writers can use their imaginations and abilities to "think outside the box" to find ideas to write about. He has created a distinctive voice, a unique style, subjects that I will cover in chapters 4 and 5.

The Writer's Need for Confidence

Confidence is important for writers. If you aren't confident about your ideas and your ability to communicate them well, your motivation for writing will suffer and you may experience writer's block, which is driven by anxiety. When necessary, of course, we write various texts (memos, letter, reports) for committees or administrators because of external pressures. But this pressure is no substitute for confidence-inspired motivation. Although many writers say they work best under pressure, generally what writers produce when pressed for time is of poor quality. For one thing, time restraints limit rewriting, and the writer doesn't have sufficient time to get any distance from what they have written.

You need to feel confident that you have something interesting or useful to say and that others will benefit from reading what you have written. If you use the tools described in this book, you can organize your time more effectively, prepare an outline that will be useful, and write in a more confident manner. One way to build confidence as a writer is to practice writing. "Practice makes perfect" is a known maxim, and while practicing might not make your writing perfect, it will help you to become a better writer if you examine your writing from a critical perspective.

The Writer's Need for Ideas

All writers need ideas. The secret for writing long texts is maintaining interest: that comes from finding a topic that you want to write about. Then do some brainstorming and play around with ideas related to your topic, ask as many questions about it as you can think of, and then answer these questions as best you can. Keeping a writer's journal is an excellent way to explore ideas that you can use in your writing; I'll discuss this more in the next section.

Another way to generate these ideas is through research. In some cases this involves writing up research you have conducted or—for reports, memos, and other texts involving the functioning of your institution—interviewing colleagues and administrators. In other cases it involves looking for information in the library or via the Internet and finding material written by authorities and experts in your subject area. The more information you have, the more ideas you can discuss and explain.

As William Zinsser explains in his superb book, *On Writing Well*:

> An . . . important moral is to look for your material everywhere, not just by reading the obvious sources and interviewing the obvious people. Look at signs and at billboards and at all the junk written along the American roadside. Reading labels on our packages and instructions on our toys, the claims on our medicines and the graffiti on our walls. (71)

Zinsser calls our attention to something important—not confining our research to the usual sources, but researching "outside the box," being open to material from unlikely sources. He also suggests that valuable information can be found everywhere if you keep your eyes open. For many years the academic community ignored popular culture, not recognizing that it contains valuable information about the culture and societies in which it is found. Now scholars in many fields are gaining information about cultures and societies from comic books, graffiti, jokes, and other aspects of popular culture.

Whenever possible, find a subject you are interested in when selecting a topic for a monograph or book. If you like the subject you are investigating, the research satisfies your curiosity and becomes a pleasure rather than a chore. In some cases, of course, you don't have the luxury of writing about a subject you are interested in but must write about a subject of interest and importance to your colleagues, editors of journals, or administrators in your institution. Even though the topic of this type of report or other document may not be of interest to you, make sure that what you write is as informative, accurate, and polished as possible—this will reflect positively on you.

The Value of Keeping a Journal

As I mentioned earlier, I've kept journals continuously since 1956. Let me mention something about journals and offer some ideas for keeping them that I think will help writers. It's in my journals that I do a lot of thinking about the books and articles I write. I write about other things as well—what the weather is like, how I'm feeling, what I think about the plays I've been to, politics, and so on. I also write in journals so that I won't forget how to write with a pen and my handwriting won't get any worse than it is already.

I make a distinction between diaries, which focus on personal relationships and tend to be private and emotional in nature, and journals. Journals may include our experiences but they are, as I see it, mainly concerned with ideas and thoughts, especially related to writing projects. It might be best to think of journals as workbooks for writers.

One important thing to know about journals is that as you write in them, your mind often brings to consciousness interesting ideas you have but weren't aware of—ideas that your writing calls up from your unconscious. And the process of writing frequently leads to new ideas and thoughts that will be useful to you. Ideas generate other ideas. When I write articles and books, I find that after I've done my writing for the day, in my journal I speculate about what I've written and think about what I'll write the next day. So the actual writing that I do on a given day is only part of the process involved in writing.

I suggest you use a bound notebook for your journals (you can find inexpensive ones at any art supply store), number the pages, and make an index of the topics covered on the last page of your journal. I number the pages of my journals (and also number and give a title to each journal) so later on I can access topics I've discussed more easily. I usually draw four lines vertically on some pages that I want to reserve for brainstorming on a subject. For example, if I'm planning to write a chapter in a book or an essay on some topic, such as cockfighting in Bali, I use the columns in my journal to play around with ideas about cockfighting and then I select some ideas from the journal to put onto slips of paper to make an outline.

I've used my journals to design courses, plan nonfiction books, plot novels, make to-do lists, make travel plans, and many other things. I set aside ten or fifteen minutes a day to write in my journals. Since I write nearly every day, I fill a journal in around eight months.

On the Usefulness of Journals: A Case History

A number of years ago, Mitch Allen, for whom I've written many books, asked me to do a comic book on postmodernism. I tried to draw the comic book but found I didn't like working under the limitations of the comic-strip format. I was speculating about these difficulties in one of my journals, volume 65, Master of Demystification (written on February 25, 1996, page 144), when an image popped into my head. It was of a man who had just been murdered,

What I could do -- with some degree of authority ??

Thurs. May 16, 1996 (RAIN)

I taught my last class ... So it's one more year down the hatch ... Number 30 ... I passed in my grades .. just have to look over some scripts -- I'm still a bit under the weather .. so I'm just resting in bed .. + taking it easy .. will do the same tomorrow ... I might do a bit of writing if I'm up to it ??

COMEDY & CODES	
COMIC ASPECT	CODE VIOLATION
Liars + Frauds	Truthfulness
Eccentrics	Normalcy
Incongruous	Flexibility
Crazies	Rationality
Obsessed	Reasonableness
Types of all sorts	Individuality + Identity
Old men who want young	Youthful love
women (sexual)	& Romance.
Braggarts &	Modesty
Negotiators	

I have to get started on the last chapter soon .. maybe tomorrow, if I'm up to it ?? I'll have to redo the index, also .. but it won't be that much work ..

I can use a break from the classroom ... and will have almost 15 weeks ... just about a semester, if you think about it .. and I didn't get sick .. except for this minor cold the last week of the semester.

I just hooked onto E-mail + I've lost all my messages .. pretty crazy ... I think that happened once before .. maybe I did something at my office with Eudora? I'll call tomorrow + see what the situation is ?? It's just one thing after another ... last time I called Susan Chin, I believe ... 338-1211. Helpdesk@sfsu.edu (Sigourney 33). I sent an E-mail message to the helpdesk and will see what happens ?? Now I'm just relaxing ... and trying to kick this cold ... What a nuisance.

150 The conjunction – Huckabee was second ... It looks like John Edwards is finished ... he hardly got any votes in the Nevada Caucus ... but who knows? Next week the Democrats have a race in South Carolina ... + we'll see what happens there ...

I revised my article yet again ... and think it's close to being okay ... I still don't have Bob's article ... there's no hurry ... Then I'll have that project taken care of ... and it will be on to the next ...

Sunday, Jan. 20, 2008 (cloudy)

Bob McKecher sent his article, on stewardship, so now I have the package ready to go ... to <u>Society</u> ... I'll send it off next week ... So that project has worked out well .. and I'll have provided <u>Society</u> with some good articles on Tourism ... That leaves only my writing book + that's up to Natalie to decide on ... what has cut and who she'll send it to for copy-editing, etc. etc. That kind of work isn't too demanding ... When I'm done with that I won't have everything in the pipeline ... and can work on some articles I've been thinking about.

THE HERO LEAVES HOME
The Traveler as Hero + The Hero as Traveler

Propp's Morphology	FUNCTIONS: Basic components of a tale	XI The HERO LEAVES HOME A 32 DEPARTURE	VII Deception – Tourist Trips
Problem + classify fairy tales	A. Story B. Not bounded C. Sequence always uniform	XIV (?) Transport various channels place themselves at the disposal of the hero	VIII Look & desire to live
Can't do themes since the story has several themes	all fairy tales are alike in terms of structure	XV The hero is Transferred	IX hero allowed to go or is deactivated
Can't do types since different not clear cut	FUNCTIONS: Initial situations then functions	XX the hero returns Two Kinds of Heroes	other traveler
Can't do motifs because motifs can be decomposed into smaller units only great way – components of tales + their relationship to one another of whole	Can adapt form to Travel Or Constraint is that all tales are Travel tales	Seekers – quest victimized + conflict can apply Propp's structural principles to Travel	Both model interlace?? Dr. Mircea Eliade in Complying myths
FUNCTIONS of characters 31 in toto	1st Function ABSENTATION	certain functions involved in Travel Basic Elements of a Trip... possible Folk Tale: chart	Bettelheim on fairy tales? COMPONENTS OF A TRIP ABROAD

slumped over a table. There was a knife in his back, a bullet hole in his head, a poison arrow in his cheek, and his drink, which had spilled, was giving off poisonous fumes.

I then wrote a paragraph that was to become the first chapter of my mystery novel *Postmortem for a Postmodernist*. Because my handwriting is difficult to read, I will translate the passage I wrote in my journal:

> When the lights went on again, the body of professor Ettore Gnocchi was slumped over on the table. A small red hole was in his forehead, from which a thin trickle of blood flowed. A knife was in his back, and the material around it was stained a dark red . . . and a long, dark arrow was lodged in his right cheek. The glass of wine he had just drank from had spilled making a large round stain on the tablecloth, from which a sulfuric mist was rising . . . curiously, a smile was frozen on his face.

The page in my journal in which I wrote this paragraph is shown on the following page. Once I had launched myself into the novel, I then spent a good amount of time writing in my journal about the proposed novel—thinking about the story I'd tell, the characters I'd use, and that kind of thing. I've reproduced one of the pages (150), which shows how I diagrammed the murder scene and worked on the various characters in the novel. So it is fair to say that *Postmortem for a Postmodernist* was born on the pages of that journal. And my nonfiction books also took shape in my journals, as I thought about topics I might want to write longer works about and how I might approach them.

The moral, then, is that if you want to develop your ability to write, keeping a journal, in which you play around with ideas and do other things, is an important tool and one that can lead to developments you might never have anticipated. The more you write, the easier it will become and the better a writer you'll become. As I mentioned earlier, in my journals I often write about what I *will* write. Then I write at the computer, based on what I wrote in my journal. Then I write in my journal about what I have written. And the process goes on and on, and as I write more books I think of yet other books to write—or find editors who have books they want me to write.

The Importance of Research

Years ago, I went to a communication conference in Boston, and while I was there I arranged to have lunch with one of my editors. (One of the pleasures of being an author is that editors sometimes take you to lunch.) I was in the middle of eating a large lobster in a nice restaurant when my editor pulled out a thick book from her briefcase and handed it to me.

144

I think my Sitcom writing class is down to 7 or 8
students... there's little chance I'll have more than that number
really a sad commentary on things... I've got to think about what
I can teach — in the way of courses — so I don't have to teach
the same course twice in one semester.. Though that isn't the end of the
world by any means...

331 ANALYSIS OF PUBLIC ARTS	270 WRITING FOR ELECT. MEDIA	576 INTERNSHIP	530 COMEDY WRITING
530 SITUATION COMEDY WRITING	331 SEMINAR IN MEDIA CRITICISM	? SEMINAR IN SITCOM WRITING	? SEMINAR IN SEMIOTIC ANALYSIS

It's the fourth course that's the problem.. but it isn't that
bothersome to teach two sections of the writing course or internship
course, if necessary... while I do my other thing.. with editors,
etc. But that may be coming to an end, as well?! I'll see... I
probably will have to revise my Seeing in Balance and I still can
do the Postmodernism book... if I can figure out how to do it..

When the lights went on again the
body of Professor Ettore Gricchi
was slumped over on the table. A small
red hole was in his forehead, from which
a thin trickle of blood flowed. A knife
was in his back, of the writing and it
was stained a dark red... and a long dart was
lodged in his right cheek. The glass of wine
he had just drank from had spilled,
making a large red stain on the
tablecloth, for which an acidy must
was rung... there was, curiously, a sulphurous
frown on his face...

That's how I'll start it.. with his being killed four or five
different ways — presumably by different people... and see what I can
do?!! I'll start with an image and see what I can figure out
to explain what happened, etc.

<u>Mon. Feb. 26, 1996</u> (Sun)

A gorgeous day.. I got up at 6:30 + had breakfast..
Then I went to the alumni Inn + led a workshop on humor
and related matters.. it seemed to go over quite well.. I came
home + the Ungers called + we're to go out to dinner. I came

150 more... Ike wants to put the whole book on the Internet... on some page on the Web ...or something like that.. he's got a connection at Sun Microsystems who probably can steer us in the right direction ??

"This book on communication research methods isn't selling well," she said. "I'd like you to take a look at it and see if you can figure out why. And by the way, we'd like you to write one on the same subject. I'd like sixty thousand words and would like to have the manuscript in eight months."

On the plane back to San Francisco, I examined the book and tried to figure out why it was not successful. When I got home, I gathered together all the books I had on media and communication research and made a list of the topics they addressed. That is, I did research—in this case, on books on communication research. I also collected syllabi from my colleagues who taught courses on research. After I had done this research, I started making an outline of the main topics that were covered in the other books. I made outlines for each chapter and spent a great deal of time trying to figure out what the order of the chapters should be and how to organize the book.

It's always best, William Zinsser advises in *On Writing Well*, to gather more information than you need:

> You should always collect more material that you will eventually use. Every article is strong in proportion to the surplus of details from which you can choose the few that will serve you best—if you don't go on gathering facts forever. At some point you must decide to stop researching and start writing. (71)

By having more information than you need, you can be picky and use only the best material for your purposes. It also can help prevent you from padding your writing—that is, writing in a wordy style. Readers are able to sense when authors are heading off on a tangent or repeating themselves for no reason.

Once you've decided on a subject for research, come up with a system to organize your research. I have a filing cabinet in which I keep clippings of articles, in manila folders, on subjects I write about. The articles often have statistics and quotations from authorities that are useful to me. I also find it useful to print out all the material I find on the Internet so I can be sure of the Internet addresses and can check that my quotations are accurate. Save all of the material that you will be using for quotations, paraphrasing, and citations. If you don't save it, you'll find yourself spending a good deal of time searching again for the same material when you need to document your sources.

What you'll discover is that when you focus on a topic, unless it is very narrow and specialized, any number of articles in newspapers and magazines on the subject will pop up. Let me offer an example. I write ethnographic tourism books and decided to write a study of tourism in Rajasthan, India, and the so-called Golden Triangle—Delhi, Agra (location of the Taj Mahal), and Jaipur. Once I began my research, I quickly found many articles in newspapers such as the *San Francisco Chronicle,* the *Wall Street Journal,* and the *New York Times* about India—and there was even a cover story on India in *Time* magazine. You also can use the Internet to find articles of interest through sites such as Google Scholar, Google, and Wikipedia. You should investigate your topic in scholarly journals as well, since journals are generally more up-to-date than books. It takes around a year to publish a book, so anything you read in a book is at least a year old.

We research all the time—when we are deciding what kind of car to purchase or where to vacation—except that this informal kind of research isn't subject to academic research rules as far as evidence and reliability are concerned. When you're writing academic works, you need to be more careful about the integrity of your sources, about being accurate when you quote others, and about making generalizations that you can support. While this book isn't about academic research, it is important to follow the common practices in your field. You can find guidelines in scholarly journals and books on research in your area of interest to help you with these matters. Unless you are writing a "think piece" or are speculating about ideas, you need to base your writing on research by reputable scholars.

As Zinsser says, you can't gather information endlessly. At some point you have to stop. Once you have done your research and have a body of factual material, data, ideas, or whatever it is you need, depending on your field, you are ready to move on to the next steps in writing—making an outline, writing a first draft, and revising that draft.

The Writing Process
Outlining, Drafting, and Revising

Almost all good writing begins with terrible first efforts. You need to start somewhere. Start by getting something—anything—down on paper. A friend of mine says that the first draft is the down draft—you just get it down. The second draft is the up draft—you fix it up. You try to say what you have to say more accurately. And the third draft is the dental draft, where you check every tooth, to see if it's loose or cramped or decayed, or even, God help us, healthy.

—Anne Lamott, *Bird by Bird*, 25–26

If, on looking over your first draft you find that your mind as reader is not satisfied with your mind as writer, change the writing and make a mental note of the sort of jumpiness that ails you in composing. No man who writes attains adequate coherence through his first draft. Everyone *must* revise, which means displace, add missing links, remove repetitions, in short, tinker. As we tinker, presumably we improve and polish.

These various operations will in time become second nature to you, but at first the tendency when reading over one's prose is to find it perfectly lucid and forceful, not to say sublime. You must therefore lay aside your manuscript for several days and return to it as if it were written by someone else. And since this may not provoke sufficient self-criticism, you must examine each statement for its accuracy of form as well as relevancy of contents.

—Jacques Barzun and Henry F. Graff, *The Modern Researcher*, 247–48

Now that we've done our research and gathered together the material we need to begin writing, let's move from thoughts and ideas to getting something down on paper. The outline is the place to start. I have a story to tell about the importance of outlines. I once asked a famous sociologist, the author of numerous articles and books, to contribute an article to a collection on tourism that I was gathering for a journal. He agreed and wrote to me, "I will make an outline and get a draft to you in a few weeks." A few weeks later he e-mailed me an article. "This is a draft," he wrote. "Please let me know if it is suitable." I replied that his article was just what I was looking for. I was very happy with what he sent me. I asked him to add some bibliographical material. Then he sent a message saying that he was going to make minor revisions to the paper and write a final draft. The moral of this story is that even famous scholars, with many articles and books to their names, make outlines. Just as you can't tell the ball players without a program, you can't write an article or a book or a text of any length without an outline.

The Art of the Outline

Years ago I went to a conference at Stanford University. The session I attended had three speakers and a moderator, who made sure things ran smoothly and offered his perspective on the speakers' presentations. Before the session began, the moderator did something curious. He took four or five pieces of 8.5-inch by 11.5-inch white paper, folded them, and tore them into halves. He then folded the halves into quarters and tore them again, and the quarters into eighths and so on, until he had a stack of two-inch by three-inch pieces of paper.

"What's this all about?" I wondered.

As the speakers gave their presentations, the moderator jotted notes, writing a single point on each slip of paper. After all the speakers had finished, the moderator took a couple of minutes to shuffle his slips of paper into order and then, referring to these slips, gave a wonderful analysis and discussion of all of the presentations.

What the moderator was doing, of course, was outlining his presentation as the speakers gave their talks. Then, after they finished, he turned those notes into a coherent outline and used that outline to structure his comments.

Since I attended that conference, I have taken to tearing up sheets of paper in the same manner to make an outline for every paper or chapter in a book that I've written. From this experience I also learned an important point about outlining: *You should put only one topic, idea, or subject on each piece of paper.* If you do this, you can easily rearrange the pieces of your outline. When I write a book, I start by making a list of the chapters that I think I will write. Then I make an outline with slips of paper representing topics for each chapter. When I'm finished with this process, I lay out all my chapters and slips of paper on the dining room table and start rearranging chapters and topics so that the book is logically constructed.

Generally, I staple the slips for each chapter together and save them in sandwich bags. I save them because I never can be sure I won't be asked to revise one of my books and want to have the slips available. Different writers approach outlining in different ways, but finding a method of outlining that works for you is important. Use your outlines—and save them in case you have need of them in the future.

Sometimes, there is no one "right" way to structure a book. For this book, for instance, I could have started with a chapter on style or genres and then written something about the writing process, but it seemed to me that general topics related to writing should go before chapters on genres of academic writing. One challenge when learning about writing is that many different things come at you "all at the same time," so to speak, so there is not a single, most logical system to follow in a book on writing. And a given topic can be discussed in a number of different places in the book, which causes more problems. But however you decide to structure your text, you should use an outline.

The advantage of making outlines is that you can see the logical structure of what you'll be writing and arrange your topics in the best possible way. Even with outlines, you sometimes find that when you start writing, it makes sense to move some material from one place to another in your manuscript. In the first version of this book, for example, I had any number of passages that were not essential, which I eliminated from later versions. But having an outline minimizes the need for such changes.

Writing a First Draft

Every writer will tell you the same thing about writing:
Writing always involves rewriting.

I suggest that when you are writing any kind of document you create a rough first draft as quickly as possible. The important thing is to get something down on paper. Anything is better than nothing—at this early stage, don't worry if what you write needs rewriting.

Watching artists at work provides a useful analogy. Artists do not start their paintings in the upper left-hand corner of their canvas and create a perfect painting as they expand from that corner to the bottom right-hand corner. Rather, they sketch in the outline of the painting and then paint here and there

on the canvas, continually changing their approach, adding colors here and there, clearing away areas on the canvas they don't like, until after much painting and repainting they have a finished picture. This is a good model for writers. You "rough in" the article or book or whatever it is you are working on, writing it as quickly as possible. Then, when you've finished your first draft, you start polishing what you have written.

Generally, I recommend you write no more than five pages (approximately 1,500 words) a day on your project. I find that if I write more than this in a day, I become so tired that I'm not able to write well the next day. Writing five pages takes me about two or three hours, sometimes longer if I'm having a hard time finding the information I need or the right way of expressing myself.

The five pages suggestion is advice for pacing yourself. If an editor asks you to write a 6,000-word essay, and you write 1,500 words a day, it will take you four days to rough in the first draft. Writing 1,500 words may not seem like very much, but when you sit at the computer to write, you may find that it takes you longer than you thought. If you have difficulty reaching 1,500 words, set yourself a limit of 1,000 words a day and take six days to write your essay. If you are writing a book, a pace of 1,000 words a day in fifty days of writing yields a 50,000-word manuscript, enough for a book.

Let me mention the importance of planning your time, pacing yourself, and setting a deadline for first drafts. I've never missed a deadline because I usually start writing my projects as soon as I get them. That allows me plenty of time to work on and revise them. Leaving writing assignments for the last moment always generates stress—and usually generates mediocre texts.

Some people are morning people and others are night people. You should schedule your writing for when you are at your best—if you're a morning person, you should do your writing in the morning. I like to write first thing in the morning, right after breakfast. Many of my colleagues assumed that, since I've written so many books, I write all day long, every day. In fact, I seldom write at the computer for more than two or three hours a day. But when I start a writing project, I write steadily—almost every day, but never for more than two or three hours each day. Of course I do spend some time every day writing in my journal, often speculating about what I've written and about new ideas or things I've left out of my draft.

It's also important to follow instructions. Writers sometimes become so excited about writing that they don't pay attention to what they've been asked to write—that is, they end up ignoring the specifications that they have been given. This leads to problems such as essays, monographs, research project write-ups, and even books that are not focused on the proper subject, aren't written in the style that is requested, or are much shorter (or much longer) than specified.

Revise Your First Drafts on Hard Copy (Printouts)

This is a matter I think is of crucial importance.

Always make your revisions on hard copy—that is, on printouts of your articles or papers or books.

Over the years I've tried, from time to time, revising my drafts at the computer, but it never works. So I've learned to make a printout of my first draft and make my revisions on that hard copy. I'm not sure why revising drafts on a computer isn't satisfactory. It may be that having a printout enables me to see errors or changes that should be made and helps me to see the entire text when reviewing organization rather than a few paragraphs at a time on a flickering screen. Whatever the reason, I find that working on a printout is important.

Once you make any changes to your draft on the hard copy, it isn't difficult to input those changes to your first draft on your computer—which means that once you've added your changes and corrections, you now have a second draft of your text. The next step is to print your second draft and read it again. You may find, for example, that you want to move certain passages in your text to a different location. You may want to add some new lines of thought. You may think of new subheads to add. There are any number of revisions you may want for this second draft.

It is possible, of course, to keep making printouts and revisions of what you've written endlessly, but at a certain point—generally by the third or fourth draft—you probably will have a work that is suitable for your needs and will most likely please anyone who has to read what you've written—assuming, that is, that your reasoning is correct and the examples you use are relevant.

The Art of the Revision

You may be able to write a decent first draft, but this draft will not be as good as your second draft, and your second draft won't be as good as your third. I usually write many drafts of my books, because I'm not satisfied with what I've written in only one or two. I write my first drafts as quickly as possible, to get my ideas down. But these first drafts, I've found, always need substantial revision. I want to change the language used here and there, find the "right" word in certain cases, or change the organization. I have the most fun making revision, for when I'm making my revisions, I feel that I'm functioning creatively. Let me offer some suggestions to follow when revising texts.

Put your word-processed draft aside for a while. It's a good idea to not look at your first draft for a couple of days after you've finished it. When you are involved with a text, your mind is so wrapped up in it that you can't recognize problems or see mistakes you've made. So put the draft aside, and later, when your mind is fresh, start working on revising it.

Check for spelling and typing errors. Usually writers make typing or spelling errors. Always use your spell-checker, keeping in mind that even a spell-checker will miss words that are spelled correctly but used incorrectly. Spell-checkers generally can't tell that "you're" should have been "your," for instance, or that

---

Suggestions for Revising Texts

Put your word-processed draft aside for a while.
Check for spelling and typing errors.
Use the word count feature in your word processing program.
Change the language you've used.
Check for punctuation errors.
Change the organization of your text.
Insert new subheads and remove superfluous ones.
Check your citations and references
Use a good format to facilitate revisions.

"to" should have been "too." Also check that you've not made errors in copying quotations. It's easy to misspell a name or leave out words. Leaving out a word can change the meaning of the quotation, so you should be especially careful when quoting other works.

Use the word count feature in your word processing program. Sometimes, such as when you're writing a book for a publisher, you are given specific word counts for your texts. Check the number of words you've written after you've finished revising your work to make sure you've not written too little or, as it often happens, too much. Every book contract I've signed has included the number of words required (or desired, if this matter is open to revision). You can also use the word count program to compare the lengths of sections or chapters to determine whether the work is balanced.

Change the language you've used. This is the most common problem in revisions, for usually you can find better language than what you've put down in your first draft. Since your use of language conveys your ideas, when you change your language you are also clarifying your thinking. Sometimes just changing a single word profoundly affects your readers' interpretation of what you've written.

Check for punctuation errors. When you're writing your first draft, and your mind is racing and thinking about a number of different things at once, it is easy to make punctuation errors. The newer word processing programs often call your attention to punctuation errors when you use the spell-checker and grammar-checker function, but you still need to review your drafts to find these errors.

Change the organization of your text. After you've finished your first draft, you may find that some material you've written in one section belongs somewhere else. Sometimes what we write doesn't fit perfectly into our outlines, and we need to rearrange segments to make the material more coherent.

Insert new subheads and remove superfluous ones. It's a good idea to use subheads (except, perhaps, in very short papers) to let your reader know what topic you'll be writing about in a section of your text. When revising, often you need to add new subheads, or you need to modify the existing ones. Each time you work on a new draft, you should review your subheads to make sure they are working to cue your readers to your discussion.

Check your citations and references. You should always check over the quoted material to make sure you haven't left out any words or skipped a line. Check for mistakes in your list of references, including the names of authors, the titles of articles and books you've used, and the publication dates and publisher information. Also, you should review your work for missing citations or reference information.

Use a good format to facilitate revisions. If you're revising on your printouts, format the margins so that there is enough space to write things down, insert new material, and make notes during the revising process. It is difficult to read long lines of type on a page because the eye gets tired. So leave substantial margins on each side of the page, not only because it will be easier on your eyes when you write, but also because it will facilitate revising and rewriting.

The writing process, I've suggested, is a very complicated one, requiring a considerable amount of discipline and attention to detail. At some point you will need to start writing a first draft, as Anne Lamott suggests. Then you will need to revise what you've written, since first drafts seldom are decent, as Jacques Barzun and Henry F. Graff argue.

Now we can turn our attention to the next topic—writing with style.

On Structure and Style

As an essay approaches the almost pure exposition of a scientific monograph, say, the personality of the writer diminishes, and properly so. The writer's concern is to set down a body of facts or ideas, logically and efficiently. The language should be precise and unemotional, transparent so that one sees through the words directly to the subject. The pronoun I is avoided, or used sparingly; tone tends to be colorless. In short, the writing is technical and usually interests only the experts.

—Thomas S. Kane and Leonard J. Peters, *Writing Prose*

Basically, I require two things of an author. The first is that he has something interesting to say—something that will either teach me or amuse me. If he doesn't, I stop reading. The second requirement is that he not waste my time getting out what he has to say. If he idles, I conclude that I can be taught quicker elsewhere.

—John R. Trimble, *Writing with Style*, 69–70

I n Benjamin Franklin's *Autobiography*, one of the most important and fascinating documents of the American revolutionary period, he writes:

> But as prose writing has been of great use to me in the course of my life, and was a principal means of my advancement, I shall tell you how, in such a situation, I acquired what little ability I have in that way . . .
>
> My father happened to find my papers and read them. Without entering into the discussion, he took occasion to talk to me about the manner of my writing; observed correct spelling and pointing. . . . I fell far short in elegance of expression, in method, and in perspicuity, the justice of his remarks, and then thence grew more attentive to the *manner* in writing, and determined to endeavor at improvement.

Prose writing, Franklin explains, was the "principal means" of his advancement, and his father, we can see, functioned as a kind of prototypical writing instructor. Franklin was, in many respects, an archetypal self-created American. You know that when you read his autobiography. Writing is also the principal means for the advancement of many people today—in places such as universities, businesses, organizations, and governmental agencies. What you will find when you do this kind of writing is that every word counts and you have to find the right words to convey your ideas correctly.

Le Mot Juste (The Exact Word)

Every word we use conveys a particular meaning and has certain connotations. We must be extremely careful, then, about our language. Just changing one word or substituting one word for another can impact the way readers interpret what is written. The French have a term, *le mot juste,* which means "the right word" or "the correct word." You have to find the "exact" word to get your ideas across and give your readers the impression you want them to have.

A paper of 2,500 words, an article of 5,000 words, or a book of 50,000 words starts with a single word. In your first draft, don't spend too much time worrying about how to start the text, about that first word. Just jump right in. If you have writer's block, think of your text as a letter you are writing to a friend and start writing that letter. Or start in the middle of your article and then, after writing for awhile, go back to the beginning.

After you have roughed in a first draft of a text, revise and polish it. This is where the process of finding the exact word comes into play, for there is a world of difference between having an acceptable word and having the right word in a text.

Each word we write represents a choice we make. In an earlier draft of this book, for example, I wrote "every word" in the previous sentence, but then I decided that writing "each word" focuses our attention more directly on particular words while "every word" deals with the totality of the words we write. The terms "each" and "every" might not seem that different, but you can see here that they have different impacts.

The words we use have denotations and connotations that must be considered when we write. The linguist George Lakoff uses the term "framing" to explain the way words and phrases mean different things to people and have different logical implications. Consider the difference between these two ways of talking about the same thing:

estate taxes
death taxes

The term "estate taxes" implies a tax on wealthy people who have "estates" and is the term generally used by Democrats. "Death taxes" suggests a tax on everyone, since everyone eventually dies, whether rich or poor. Republicans, who are good at framing issues, have taken to calling "estate taxes" by the second term, "death taxes," to argue for a repeal of these taxes that would largely benefit for wealthy people, who tend to be Republicans. So, as this example shows, the words we use often have profound social, cultural, and political implications that we must consider when we use them, because if we're not careful, we may unwittingly insult and negatively stereotype all kinds of people.

Academic writing should always use gender-neutral language. Conventional practice now deals with gender by using plurals instead of repeating "he or she." Let me offer an example: Instead of writing "When considering the reader, you must think about how he or she will respond . . . ," write "When considering your readers, you must think about how they will respond. . . . " You don't want to use "he" in such situations, because it is too gender specific and leaves out women. Likewise, it is awkward to repeat "he or she" each time.

Correcting your drafts on printouts, a tool I recommended earlier, is extremely useful in this regard. You can see words that need to be changed more clearly on printouts than you can on a computer monitor.

Fortunately, you don't have to spend a great deal of mental effort worrying about each word you choose because your mind works quickly, but remember that each and every word you use is one that you've selected from a variety of other words you could have used. Think of chefs adding spices and other ingredients to dishes to give them the right flavor. Chefs have to decide: Do I add garlic, thyme, olive oil, or something else? Writers use words the way chefs use spices and other ingredients. When I start revising my drafts, I pay special attention to the words I've used and speculate about whether, in a certain place, a different word would be more precise to the meaning and feeling I desire. I also work hard to write economically.

Strunk and White have a wonderful passage about wordy writing in *The Elements of Style*. In a section titled "Omit Needless Words," they write:

> Vigorous writing is concise. A sentence should contain no unnecessary words, a paragraph no unnecessary sentences, for the same reason that a drawing should have no unnecessary lines and a machine no unnecessary parts. This requires not that the writer make all his sentences short, or that he avoid all detail and treat all his subjects only in outline, but that every word tell. (17)

For instance, instead of writing "I am of the opinion that" we can write "I believe" or "I think" and save four words. Strunk and White give several examples of padding, which is one of the most common problems found in academic writing.

Notice Strunk and White's style—how they use different sentence lengths and analogies to make their argument. I will discuss these topics in more detail in this chapter and the next.

The Thesis Statement

When you write a text in an academic setting, in many cases you primarily will be providing information, but often you also will be proposing and defending an idea or thesis and offering a conclusion about the topic. These works are not mystery stories; you should tell your readers what conclusions you reached at the *beginning* of your text, not at the end.

So you must start with a thesis statement, which I define as your conclusion based upon your research. A thesis can be understood to be an assertion; this assertion must be supported by evidence that a reasonable person would accept.

You can think of a thesis statement as being similar in nature to the cases prosecutors present during a trial. During the opening statement to the jury, prosecutors explain the crime the defendant has been accused of committing, what laws are involved, then provide an overview of the case they will make to prove their conclusion. In this analogy, the judge and jury are equivalent to the professors or administrators or editors who will read your text, and the prosecutors' conclusion is equivalent to your conclusion—based on the results of your research—which you are previewing in your thesis statement.

The Structure and Function of Paragraphs

A book is made up of chapters, and a chapter—which you can think of as somewhat like an essay on one aspect of a topic—is made up of paragraphs. Paragraphs are made up of sentences and sentences are made up of words, which I've already addressed in my discussion of *le mot juste*. So let's look more closely at paragraphs.

In principle, each paragraph should address one thought, one idea; thus each paragraph should contain a *topic statement* to orient the reader. The remainder of the paragraph should offer details, examples, qualifications, and other material related to this topic sentence.

Paragraphs also create structure. In her book *Narrative Analysis*, Catherine Kohler Riessman discusses the work of a linguistics scholar, W. Labov, which concentrates on the organization of conversations. There are certain codes, or rules, people observe when they converse, just as there are codes writers must observe (grammar is one of the most important) if they are to effectively communicate their ideas. Riessman writes:

> Like weight bearing walls, personal narratives depend on certain structures to hold them together. Stories told in conversation share common parameters, although they may be put together in contrasting ways and, as a result, point to different interpretations. Events become meaningful because of their placement in a narrative.
>
> Labov's . . . structural approach is paradigmatic. . . . Narratives, he argues, have formal properties and each has a function. A "fully formed" one includes six common elements: an abstract (summary of the substance of the narrative), orientation (time, place, situation, participants), complicating action (sequence of events), evaluation (significance and

meaning of the action, attitude of the narrator), resolution (what finally happened), and coda (returns the perspective to the present). With these structures, a teller constructs a story from a primary experience and interprets the significance of events in clauses and embedded evaluations. (18–19)

Labov's ideas about the structure of conversations apply to all expository or academic writing. Whatever kind of document we are writing, unless it is extremely short, we should offer, in various places:

- an **abstract** that gives a summary of one's paper, early in the document
- an **orientation** offering details about the time and place of the research
- a **complicating action report** that tells how the research was conducted, including what methodology was used
- an **evaluation** of the problems faced in the research
- a **resolution** or, in this case, conclusions reached
- a **coda** or statement about the relevance of the research to the problem.

Labov's theory deals with the way the mind works, so his ideas about conversation can be applied to written texts as well. Think of an academic paper as a conversation between a writer and an imagined reader. Also, just as in conversations, writers need to recognize their need to address the codes their audiences have learned (generally the process is unconscious) about what to expect when reading a text. Paragraphs take care of these requirements for us.

Sometimes paragraphs summarize what has been covered. This helps remind your readers what they have learned and functions as a means of reinforcement. You can also offer a summary of approaches you will be taking in the rest of the text.

When I write mysteries, I make sure that, at certain points in the novel, one of the characters (usually the detective) summarizes what has taken place thus far, usually while talking with his assistant or one or more of the suspects. I include these summaries so that my readers will remember what has happened so far and so I can insert clues and point fingers at "red herrings" (false suspects or clues that divert attention from the real criminal). The main point to remember about summaries is that you must be judicious in using them and find places where they fit logically.

So paragraphs serve many purposes along with carrying on the basic function of offering information and building our argument. If a scholarly article is a building, paragraphs can be seen as bricks and transitions as the mortar that holds the bricks together.

Using Transitions

Transitions are devices by which we guide readers from one idea or segment of writing to another. We use them in sentences and between sentences (to avoid choppy writing), between paragraphs, and between sections of our papers. In a book, we may use them between chapters or parts. Transitions are cues to our thinking. In the chart below I offer some basic transitional words and phrases.

Sequences	Examples	Contrasting Notions
first	for example	but
next	for instance	in contrast
furthermore	to show this	nevertheless
to begin with	as an illustration	
Time Relations	**Causes**	**Argument Continues**
before	because	furthermore
after	since	in addition
at the same time	this leads to	to continue
meanwhile	thus	moreover
Meaning	**Effects**	**Conclusions**
this means	therefore	therefore
this suggests	accordingly	thus
this implies	as a result	we find, then
we find, then	the consequence is	to sum up

Basic Kinds of Transitions

We use transitions to lead our readers by the hand and to point out to them the meaning of what we have written or will be writing. If you do not provide enough transitions, your readers will struggle to figure out what the relevance of a passage. When you use transitions, your readers better follow your line of thinking. Thus, if you write "on the other hand," your reader knows you are giving an alternate perspective. When you write, "to continue," your reader knows you are adding to a line of reasoning.

Sometimes we use sentences or paragraphs as transitions. We may offer a summary of what we have written, and perhaps tried to demonstrate, and then use one of the transitional devices to move on to the next step in our argument.

Using Subheads

Subheads (sometimes called A-heads) announce the subject matter of the following section to your readers. In essence, subheads show the logical structure of a body of writing and are similar in function to signs along the highway that tell us where we are and where we are headed.

Writers should show the structure of their papers, and subheads are conventionally the signposts to this structure. Keep in mind that too many subheads can become irritating. Subheads should be saved for general topics and not used at the paragraph level. Also, when possible, avoid going down a level and using sub-subheads (sometimes called B-heads, C-heads, etc.), since doing so generally makes it harder for the reader to follow.

When you create subheads, consider the conventions of the genre in which you are writing and any stylistic guidelines and conventions of a particular journal to which you plan to submit an article. Read a number of articles in the journal in which you hope to publish and see how the articles use subheads and whether there are any standard subheads used in all articles, such as "introduction" and "literature review." In writing subheads for books, you can often be as imaginative and entertaining as you want to be.

There Are Many Different Styles You Can Use

French writer Raymond Queneau wrote a remarkable book, *Exercises in Style,* in which he first wrote a short passage about a young man with a long neck on a bus in Paris, and then rewrote it in more than sixty different styles. I've already offered examples of one style of writing—that used in college bulletins, which tends to be brief and telegraphic in nature. Below I briefly list and describe a number of common writing styles:

biblical	archaic language, uses "thee" and "thou"
bureaucratic	formal and impersonal
clichés	full of well-known overused phrases
dialects	Russian, Italian, French, German, and so on
discursive	goes off on tangents all the time
exclamatory	excited
hyper-Latinate	multisyllabic in nature
ideological	uses left-wing or right-wing clichés
intellectual	high level of abstraction, jargon-filled
jargonistic	uses specialized language in some field of endeavor
journalistic	uses who, what, where, when, why, how formula
legalistic	contractual, party of the first part, and so on

metaphorical	uses analogies and similes (with "like" or "as")
paradoxical	full of contradictions and seeming illogicalities
philosophical	highly abstract, often with convoluted sentences
poetic	lyrical in nature
primer	short sentences not connected to one another
psychotic	delusional, offers evidence of madness
rap	rhyming verse with a strong beat
scientific	objective, data-rich, impersonal
slang	uses unconventional language
technocratic	full of scientific jargon about devices, processes
telegraphic	skips words to get ideas across

These are only a few of the styles available to writers. Writers do not always consciously decide to use one or another of these styles; in many cases, without being aware of it, they adopt a style and use it for most of their writing. Let's read a few examples from Queneau's *Exercises in Style* that will give you an idea of how a text can be written many different ways.

Official Letter Style (21)
I beg to advise you of the following facts of which I happened to be the equally impartial and horrified witness. Today, at roughly twelve noon, I was present on the platform of a bus which was proceeding up the rue de Courcelles . . .

Dream (54)
I had the impression that everything was misty and nacreous around me with multifarious and indistinct apparitions, among whom however was one figure that stood out fairly clearly which was that of a young man whose too-long neck . . .

Cross-Examination Style (27)
—At what time did the 12:23 P.M. S-line bus proceeding in the direction of Port de Champerret arrive on that day?
—At 12.38 P.M.
—Were there many people on the aforesaid S bus?
—Bags of 'em

Queneau demonstrates that we have many stylistic choices available when we decide to write—even something as simple as a description of a young man on a bus in Paris.

Making Your Writing More Accessible

One technique to help your readers in all circumstances is to write in an accessible style. My writing style has often been described as accessible, meaning one that my readers are able to understand easily and that they generally find interesting and entertaining. I've developed this style of writing over the years—and I've been writing for more than forty years.

Let me offer some suggestions that will help you write in a more accessible and more interesting style. Generally, when you write something in an academic setting, you will be writing the kind of text that must follow certain academic conventions. But you still have a great deal of latitude to use techniques that make a text readable and accessible.

Suggestions for Writing in an Accessible Style:

Vary your sentence length and structure.
Write clearly, in an articulate and easily comprehended manner.
Avoid jargon to the extent it is possible.
Move up and down the "ladder of abstraction."
Use narratives when they will be helpful.
Provide your readers with new ideas and fascinating information—that is, be interesting.
Offer data that explain trends.
Solve practical problems.
Build on what your readers know.
Keep away from the cliché.
Be careful with humor.
Make your paper's structure show.
Use repetition wisely.

Vary your sentence length and structure. Avoid choppy writing, full of short sentences that aren't connected to one another, and also avoid the other extreme—writing very long and convoluted sentences with endless clauses. Also remember to vary your sentence structure throughout the text. Writing all your sentences with the same structure is as boring as incoherent, primer-style writing.

In his book *On Philosophical Style,* philosopher Brand Blanshard discusses a style often described as "primer-style" or "choppy" writing—numerous short sentences that are not joined together adequately. This style resembles the writing in books for young children who are learning to read. Writers must consider the length of each sentence they write, using variety and putting together their ideas in reasoned and logical ways.

> [E]ach sentence should carry the thought one step forward. But what is to count as one step? A sentence at its simplest makes one statement, but if we were to make only one statement per sentence, our writing would be unbearable. "Sir John came out of his house. He wore a top hat. He wore a monocle. He wore spats. He carried a cane. He hailed a taxi." Intolerable! When details all hang together to make one picture, they can be grasped without difficulty as forming a single unit, and we throw them together in one sentence: "Sir John, radiant in morning dress, with top hat, monocle, spats, and cane, emerged from his door and hailed a taxi." But in regions of difficulty, it is a test of literary skill to know and to take into account the length of the reader's stride. The ideal is a row of stepping-stones just far enough apart to enable him to keep moving without compelling him to make hops, skips, and jumps, still less leaps in the dark. (51–52)

Blanshard offers us an analogy: Sentences are like stepping-stones, and the writer determines how large to make them and how far apart he should place them. It is crucial to vary the length of your sentences to keep your readers alert and interested.

Write clearly, in an articulate and easily comprehended manner. Writing clearly involves expressing ideas in a way that is easy to follow and using language that is neither ambiguous nor confusing.

In *On Writing Well*, William Zinsser offers us an analogy that all writers should keep in mind. Reading nonfiction, he suggests, is like walking along a path. The writer functions as the reader's guide, and if the writer has been a careless guide, the reader inevitably will get lost:

> If the reader is lost, it is generally because the writer has not been careful enough to keep him on the path.
>
> This carelessness can take any number of forms. Perhaps a sentence is so excessively cluttered that the reader, hacking his way through the verbiage, simply doesn't know what it means. Perhaps a sentence has been so shoddily constructed that the reader could read it in any of several ways. Perhaps the writer has switched pronouns in mid-sentence, or has switched tenses, so the reader loses track of who is talking or when the action takes place. Perhaps Sentence B is not a logical sequence to Sentence A—the writer, in whose head the connection is clear, has not bothered to provide

the missing link. Perhaps the writer has used an important word incorrectly by not taking the trouble to look it up. He may think that "sanguine" and "sanguinary" mean the same thing, but the difference is a bloody big one. The reader can only infer (speaking of big differences) what the writer is trying to imply. (9, 12)

Zinsser makes an important point. All writers struggle to write clearly and get their ideas across. We might write in a careless manner in our first drafts, but if we rewrite these drafts, chances are we'll avoid many careless errors and take care to polish our writing so it sparkles.

But what is "unclear" writing? Zinsser lists these characteristics:

- writing cluttered sentences
- writing poorly constructed sentences
- writing sentences with a confusing use of language
- switching pronouns and verb tenses without warning
- thinking in an illogical and confused manner
- using words incorrectly
- avoiding awkward, grammatically incorrect, constructions

Avoid jargon to the extent it is possible. If you are writing about Freudian psychoanalytic theory, you can't help but use the terms appropriate to that theory. Thus, you can't avoid using terms such as the Oedipus complex, castration anxiety, the id, the ego, and the superego. If you do use technical terms and jargon, define the terms and explain how you are using them so your readers can understand you.

Consider the two passages below. The first is from Walter Buckley's *Sociology and Modern Systems Theory* and the second is from *Cultural Theory*, a book by Michael Thompson, Richard Ellis, and Aaron Wildavsky.

> Rappoport and Horwatch go on to suggest that two classes of conceptual tools were needed to extend "systematic rigorous theoretical methods" to the organized complexity of the holist. Both of these derive from the older biological methods of teleology and taxonomy. 1) The old teleology has been made respectable by cybernetics, which appeals directly to physical laws and principles governing the construction of networks of causal relations, including closed-loop "feedbacks," which made possible an acceptable operational definition of goal-seeking behavior without true teleology. 2) The distinction between machines with and without the feedback loops that make for goal-seeking is a *topological* distinction, definable in terms of graph theory, a branch of topology. (38)

This passage requires a considerable amount of knowledge of systems theory and other somewhat esoteric fields to understand. Let me contrast that with a passage found in *Cultural Theory*. In their book, Thompson, Ellis, and Wildavsky deal with a social anthropologist, Mary Douglas, who has a theory about what she calls Grid-Group relationships. The authors explain "grid" and "group as follows:

> She argues that the variability of an individual's involvement in social life can be adequately captured by two dimensions of sociality: group and grid. *Group* refers to the extent to which an individual is incorporated into bounded units. The greater the incorporation, the more individual choice is subject to group determination. *Grid* denotes the degree to which an individual's life is circumscribed by externally imposed prescriptions. The more binding and extensive the scope of the prescriptions, the less of life that is open to individual negotiation. (5)

This passage explains the terms in a clear and easy-to-understand manner. A considerable part of academic writing, as you can see from the two examples I've cited, involves explaining how certain terms are to be defined and applied.

Let me offer two other examples. The first one is from the Bible and is written in a poetic manner using simple words. The second, by George Orwell (on bureaucratic rendering of Ecclesiastes passage) from "Politics and the English Language," tells the same story but uses bureaucratic and Latinate jargon to do so.

> I returned and saw under the sun, that the race is not to the swift, nor the battle to the strong, neither yet bread to the wise, nor yet riches to men of understanding, nor yet favor to men of skill; but time and chance happeneth to them all. (Ecclesiastes 9:11)

> Objective consideration of contemporary phenomena compels the conclusion that success or failure in competitive activities exhibits no tendency to be commensurate with innate capacity, but that a considerable element of the unpredictable must invariably be taken into account.

Move up and down the "ladder of abstraction." The "ladder of abstraction" covers everything from the concrete and specific (Bessie is a cow) to lofty abstractions (generalizations about all animals or all living things). Writing that is too heavily focused on details becomes tedious, and so does writing that is uniformly abstract.

Use narratives when they will be helpful. Narratives are stories, and through stories, as I explained earlier, people learn things. In writing academic prose, although your main thrust will be on ideas, insert relevant narratives, explanations, descriptions, and other devices to make your text more readable and interesting.

Provide your readers with new ideas and fascinating information—that is, be interesting. People often say "interesting" when they don't know how to respond to something they read or hear and don't want to take a position. I understand the term "interesting" to mean:

- offering surprising factual information
- discussing and explaining new ideas your reader may not know
- pointing out unrecognized relationships among phenomena

If you want people to read what you've written, take pains to make it worth their while by giving them rewards, such as those listed above.

Offer data that explain trends. Statistics are most useful when they have a historical or a comparative dimension to them. To learn that the average person in the United States in 2007 watched four hours of television a day is interesting, but it's more interesting if additional data shows that the average person watched two hours a day in 1997 or six hours a day in 1997. It also helps to have comparative statistics to put the figures in a broader context—for instance, to compare television viewing in the United States, Japan, Great Britain, Italy, and other countries.

Solve practical problems. Have you ever noticed how carefully people read guidebooks? Guidebooks are full of valuable information about hotels to stay in (or avoid), good restaurants to eat in, places to go, and other things to see and do. Suppose you decided to spend a few weeks in the Greek islands. Which islands should you visit? Where should you stay? What activities are available on the various islands? When you need good advice from experts, chances are you will pay attention to their recommendations. Similarly, when you are interested in a subject, you will find articles to be of great utility. For example, if you are interested in political advertising, articles on framing and other aspects of the subject, as found in scholarly journals and books, will be of great value to you. If you are writing on the topic, you should likewise offer information of practical value to your field that also has implications for further research.

Build on what your readers know. When you write, always keep your target audience in mind, and one part of doing so involves assumptions you make about what your readers already know. If they don't know much about your subject, define your terms and explain the concepts you use. One common error writers make is to assume that readers know what's in the writers' minds. Don't write in a manner that leaves important information out and doesn't explain concepts or define terms when you should do so.

Keep away from the cliché. Clichés are stock phrases that are so overused they become irritating. Many academics fall into the habit of using clichés such as "vehemently opposed," "far-reaching implications," or "categorically deny" in their writing. Avoid using clichés whenever possible.

Be careful with humor. It's perfectly acceptable to use humor but be careful that your humor is not offensive to any group or doesn't trivialize your subject matter. Remember this: humor is always risky. It can be used to make an important point or give an amusing example. But it can also disturb and antagonize some readers. The rule for humor should be this: when in doubt, leave it out.

In some cases, such as reports and applications, where seriousness is required, humor isn't called for. For example, if you are writing a letter that does not support awarding tenure to a candidate, it is inappropriate to adopt a light, humorous tone.

One problem you face with humor is that readers may not think that what you wrote was funny. In addition, there is often an aggressive and hostile aspect to humor, and writers should be careful not to inadvertently offend their readers. If you do wish to use humor in your writing, I suggest you not tell jokes (or try to adapt jokes) but use humor that fits with your personality. Some of the more common techniques are wordplay, allusions, exaggeration, and self-deprecating humor—that is, insults directed against yourself—though you must be careful that people don't take you seriously when you poke fun at yourself and think you are confessing to being incompetent. Another excellent way of injecting humor in a text is to use humorous quotations that are relevant to your subject.

If you are writing about stereotypes, the following joke might be of use:

There is a shipwreck and two men end up on a desert island. If the two men are French, one marries the woman and the other becomes her lover. If they are English, nothing happens because they haven't been introduced. If they are Russian, they send a note to Moscow in a bottle asking for instructions.

This joke deals with stereotypes we have of different nationalities, but it is inoffensive and so can be used to inject a bit of humor into a discussion of that topic.

Make your paper's structure show. It's important to guide your reader by making the organizational structure of your paper visible. You can do this by your use of summaries, subheads, and transitions. Explain to your reader what you'll be writing about early in your paper and clarify the paper's organization. Your paper shouldn't be a mystery to your reader. You don't want your reader to wonder, "What's going on here?" if you're writing expository prose.

Use repetition wisely. There is a value to repetition used to emphasize an important point and not just used to add verbiage to your texts. Repetition is purposeful reinforcement, but you must be very careful not to overdo it. In some cases, the repetition of a certain word or a particular phrase or sentence structure is used for dramatic effect, which explains why orators often use repetition.

But some writers, without being aware of it, repeat themselves needlessly by writing the same thing again and again in several different ways. Readers quickly spot this. This unconscious repetition is the kind you sometimes find in student papers. If students don't have enough ideas or information, they end up writing the same thing several different ways to fulfill the word requirements of their assignments.

I've just offered a number of techniques to keep in mind to make your writing more accessible and more interesting. It takes practice to develop a distinctive style as a writer, so don't be discouraged if your early attempts aren't always successful. When people first start riding a bike, they find it very difficult to keep their balance. But after a while, it becomes second nature. The same applies to writing. If you are aware of the tools you can use, and you practice using them, you've taken the first steps toward developing a readable and distinctive style of writing.

Developing Your Personal Voice

Anything you write will be a reflection of your personality—there's no avoiding it. So you should learn to develop a style of writing that serves your needs and reflects your personality in the most positive light. For some texts, of course, you want to avoid writing in a manner that calls attention to itself and you need to suppress your "voice."

Some scholars make a distinction between *what* someone writes and *how* they write it—between form and content. I would suggest the two are connected. The way you write affects what you write and how people react to it. In some cases, you must write in a formal manner, such as when you are writing proposals and similar professional documents. But there are other documents in which you can inject your personality and voice. Therefore it is useful and effective to develop a distinctive style.

Personal style can hold the reader's attention. As John R. Trimble writes in *Writing with Style*:

> [W]hat I find most appealing in a writer is an authentic personal manner. I like to see him come across as a living, companionable human being, not as an emotional eunuch or a stuffed shirt. I like to have an author *talk* to me, unbend to me, speak right out to me. . . . What I'm saying, I guess, is that I like an author to be himself, warts and all. It shows me that he trusts me with his vulnerability, isn't afraid of me, and isn't afraid of himself either. (70)

Trimble is writing about voice—what makes a writer's style distinctive. If writers are going to ask people to spend some time with what they've written, Trimble suggests that they have an obligation to make it worthwhile for their readers. Writers should avoid what Trimble calls "idling" and not adopt a style that is devoid of personality. Think, for example, of the fabulous passage about Delhi written by Jan Morris in her book *Destinations*, which I quoted earlier in the book. Morris has a distinctive "voice," which helps explain her great popularity with readers of travel literature. The same applies to all great writers. All writers, I suggest, should search for their voice and use it to enhance their writing.

Now that I've discussed various aspects of stylistic writing and the importance of a writer's voice, let me move on to another related matter—using rhetorical devices to make our writing more readable and, in some cases, more persuasive.

Composing Strategies

Style takes its final shape more from attitudes of mind than from principles of composition, for, as an elderly practitioner once remarked, "Writing is an act of faith, not a trick of grammar." This moral observation would have no place in a rule book were it not that style is the writer, and therefore what a man is, rather than what he knows, will at last determine his style.

—William Strunk Jr. and E.B. White, *The Elements of Style*, 77

The Father
But don't you see that the whole trouble lies here. In words, words. Each one of us has within him a whole world of things, each man of us his own special world. And how can we ever come to an understanding if I put in the words I utter the sense and value of things as I see them; while you, who listen to me must inevitably translate them according to the conception of things each of you has within himself. We think we understand each other, but we never really do.

—Luigi Pirandello, *Six Characters in Search of an Author*

This chapter looks at a few of what I call "composing strategies" for our writing. While there are numerous such aids and devices you can use, I will focus here on clarifying our ideas and providing information to our readers, using language creatively and avoiding common logical fallacies.

Clarifying Ideas

Some means of clarifying ideas include using contrasts and comparisons, definitions and examples. Let's take a look.

Contrast and Comparison

Using contrasts and comparisons is an important tool for getting our ideas across to others in a clear and understandable manner. The Swiss linguist Ferdinand de Saussure explained why the mind tends to function in terms of contrasts and oppositions. As he wrote in his book *Course in General Linguistics*, "in language there are only differences" (1966:120). He also explained, "concepts are purely differential and defined not by their positive content but negatively by their relations with other terms in the system" (117). In essence, we know a concept's meaning by knowing what it doesn't mean, by knowing its opposite. This explains why in order to understand concepts, our minds think in terms of oppositions. We know *poor* because it is the opposite of *rich*; we know *sad* because it is the opposite of *happy*. These oppositions must be related or tied to something they have in common. In the examples offered above, the common ties are wealth (rich and poor) and mental state (happy and sad).

So writers often use comparisons and oppositions to clarify ideas. Consider this passage from Robert Lifton's essay "Who Is More Dry? Heroes of Japanese Youth, "from *History and Human Survival* :

> In postwar Japan, especially among young people, it is good to be "dry" (or *durai)* rather than "wet" (or *wetto*). This means—in the original youth language, as expanded by the mass media—to be direct, logical, to the point, pragmatic, casual, self-interested, rather than polite, evasive, sentimental, nostalgic, dedicated to romantic causes, or bound by obligation in human relations; to break out of the world of cherry blossoms, haiku, and moon-viewing into a modern era of bright sunlight, jazz, and Hemingway (who may be said to have been the literary god of dryness). Intellectual youth, of course, disdain these oversimplified categories. But they too have made the words *durai* and *wetto* (typical examples of postwar

Japanized English) part of their everyday vocabulary, and they find dry objects of admiration in an interesting place: in American films about cowboys and gunmen. (104).

Lifton discusses the concept of "dryness" in Japanese culture and helps readers make sense of it by contrasting its opposite, "wetness." We can make a chart in which we see the oppositions in Lifton's text more clearly:

Dry	Wet
young	old
direct	evasive
logical	romantic
to the point	polite
pragmatic	sentimental
self-interested	bound by obligations
sunlight	moon viewing
Hemingway	haiku

It is the nature of language, Saussure suggests, that makes us use contrasts and comparisons. They are one of the most commonly used methods of explaining concepts, and, in particular, showing how two things differ. In my writing, I often use charts of contrasts and comparisons and then explain them in more detail in material that follows my charts.

Definitions and Examples

Words can have a number of definitions and meanings, and at times this confuses readers. So always explain how you define or understand a term. This is particularly important when you are discussing concepts with which your reader may not be familiar. Define the concept and, when possible, offer examples of how it should be used. For example, when using the term "sign," which has many meanings, write something like: "The term sign, as I interpret it (or "as used here") means anything that can be used to stand for something else."

Examples help writers make important points, and while an example may not prove the case, it does help readers make sense of ideas that the writer has been developing. Let me offer one example—of an example—here. Sociologists often write about "latent" and "manifest" functions. Latent function involves hidden and unrecognized aspects of human action, while manifest function involves action that is purposefully done and has recognized functions. If I leave things here and don't offer examples, you are left with abstractions and definitions. Something is lacking. You may know how to define "latent" and "manifest" functions, but you don't have a concrete notion of how they work, how they affect our behavior. So to help clarify my definitions, I add a specific example: manifest and latent functions of going to a political rally.

Young men and women might attend a political rally for a given political party because they believe in the political ideology of that party. That would be a manifest function of attending the rally. One latent function would be attending the rally with the hope that they might make the acquaintance of someone with whom to establish a romantic relationship. There can be many different latent functions involved in any of our actions. According to the social scientists, the latent functions of our behaviors—the ones we are unaware of—are generally the most interesting and important. Giving this example helps readers better understand how manifest and latent functions work.

It's always helpful to your readers to offer examples. When you offer examples of how some concept works in "the real world," your readers gain a better idea of what the concept means. Examples, we might say, put meat on the bone of theory and move from theory to practice.

Presenting Information

Some common ways of presenting information to your readers include using graphics, charts, tables, and lists, creating classification schemes, and using quotations by experts and authorities to support your ideas. Let me offer a few suggestions for each of these.

Using Graphics, Charts, Tables, and Lists

Over the years I've created a good deal of artwork for my publications, as I have for this book. I drew illustrations for the *Journal of Communication* for a dozen years and have completed many drawings for the interiors and covers of books. Drawings, charts (sometimes called figures), and other forms of graphic communication help readers better understand your writing—especially when there are contrasts and comparisons you've made—by appealing to the visual aspect of their brains. This helps reinforce ideas and concepts that you've explained using text.

Earlier in this chapter, I made a chart of the "dry" and "wet" oppositions discussed by Robert Lifton. Charts organize ideas and information in a visually arresting and easy-to-understand manner. I love including charts and tables in my writing because they permit me to show relationships among phenomena—ideas, concepts, data—graphically. You can see from the chart of the Lifton passage that the ideas buried in the text become easier to recognize and compare when presented in this way. So when you are writing about complicated ideas and relationships, consider using charts to help clarify ideas for your readers.

In many of my books I use the following chart, which I created to suggest the various focal points that one might consider in analyzing mass-mediated communication.

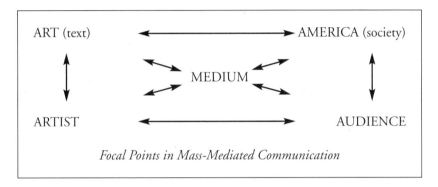

Focal Points in Mass-Mediated Communication

By looking at this chart and noting the arrows going both ways among all the focal points, a reader can visualize immediately that each element in the chart is connected, either directly or indirectly, with the others.

The same applies to tables, which spatially organize material so your reader can see how phenomena relate to one another. Tables are particularly useful for numerical data. If the data are buried in a paragraph, the reader has to work harder to recognize the significance of the data and how they relate to one another.

A list is a simple chart. Lists enable you to point out topics you are writing about in an easy-to-follow way, giving the items in your list more visibility or emphasis. I have used lists in this book, though in many cases I've not simply listed topics but also annotated them—that is, discussed them in detail. A table of contents in a book or report functions as a list of topics that will be covered. And glossaries are annotated lists, in which authors list concepts alphabetically and define them.

When creating lists, decide on a principle of organization. Some lists are organized alphabetically; others are organized according to logic, time, or another rationale. Some writers use numbers or bullets in front of the items in the list. Whichever typographic technique you use, be sure that the list helps your reader understand the points you are making. Generally, it's wise to annotate your lists and explain, even briefly, what the concepts or terms listed mean and why they are important. Items on a list should be similar in grammatical or sentence structure to be easily understood.

For instance, say I would like to change the following sentence into a list: "In the previous chapter, I dealt with topics relating to writing style, such as writing in a readable manner, employing different styles of writing, and developing your voice as a writer." I could write instead:

In the previous chapter, I dealt with topics relating to writing style, such as:

- writing in a readable manner
- employing different styles of writing
- developing your voice as a writer

Notice that the items in the list have the same grammatical structure. This helps your reader better follow your argument. In addition to lists and charts, you can use other visual tools such as photographs, drawings, and pie charts—depending on the nature of the material with which you are dealing.

Creating Classifications

Classifications fit phenomena with shared characteristics into patterns. We classify in order to organize data, ideas, or concepts and to get a sense of how they relate to one another. For example, several years ago I did a content analysis of techniques of humor found in joke books, humorous plays, comic strips, and comic books—whatever I could find that was humorous.

My interest was in seeing if I could find the basic techniques that are used to generate humor in texts of all kinds. As a result of my research, I came up with forty-five techniques of humor that are, I suggest, the building blocks of all humor. In the list below, I alphabetized the techniques and then numbered them.

1. Absurdity	16. Embarrassment	31. Parody
2. Accident	17. Exaggeration	32. Puns
3. Allusion	18. Exposure	33. Repartee
4. Analogy	19. Facetiousness	34. Repetition
5. Before/After	20. Grotesque	35. Reversal
6. Bombast	21. Ignorance	36. Ridicule
7. Burlesque	22. Imitation	37. Rigidity
8. Caricature	23. Impersonation	38. Sarcasm
9. Catalogue	24. Infantilism	39. Satire
10. Chase Scenes	25. Insults	40. Scale, Size
11. Coincidence	26. Irony	41. Slapstick
12. Comparison	27. Literalness	42. Speed
13. Definition	28. Mimicry	43. Stereotypes
14. Disappointment	29. Mistakes	44. Theme and Variation
15. Eccentricity	30. Misunderstanding	45. Unmasking

After looking over my list, I recognized that the forty-five techniques could be classified into four categories, according to whether they primarily involved language, logic, identity, or a fourth category that I called action (but which might better be called visual humor). These four categories are listed below with the techniques that fit under each category.

Language	Logic	Identity	Action
Allusion	Absurdity	Before/After	Chase scenes
Bombast	Accident	Burlesque	Slapstick
Definition	Analogy	Caricature	Speed
Exaggeration	Catalogue	Eccentricity	
Facetiousness	Coincidence	Embarrassment	
Insults	Comparison	Exposure	
Infantilism	Disappointment	Grotesque	
Irony	Ignorance	Imitation	
Literalness	Mistakes	Impersonation	
Misunderstanding	Repetition	Mimicry	
Puns/Wordplay	Reversal	Parody	
Repartee	Rigidity	Scale	
Ridicule	Theme & Var.	Stereotype	
Sarcasm	Unmasking		
Satire			

By classifying the techniques into categories, I got a better idea of how the different techniques related to one another and obtained some valuable insights into the nature of humor itself. So classification is an important tool for making sense of things—it is not an idle, intellectually interesting, exercise. When classifying, make sure that each item fits into only one category (we might call this the principle of selectivity). Also include all the items in the group of things being classified (we might call this the principle of comprehensiveness).

Quoting Authorities and Experts

Offering quotations from relevant authorities and experts in the subject you are investigating is another useful tool. Authorities and experts can provide factual data, theories, critiques, and other material to strengthen your argument. But be certain first that your authorities and experts are legitimate and that they are making statements or writing about subjects about which they are competent.

Sometimes authorities write in such a way as to make a powerful impression. When you use authorities, remember to do the following:

- Give their names
- Give the title of the article or name of the book where you found the quote
- Give the date when the article or book was published
- Give the page numbers for the material you quoted
- Check over the quoted material to make sure you have not made any careless typing errors
- Introduce the quotation by saying something about its importance and relevance to your text, or do this after the quotation.

Appeals to authority are useful, but authorities frequently disagree with one another, so a text based only on quotations from authorities is never satisfactory. Papers or works of that nature, which are just strings of quotations following one another, are undesirable because your voice, as an author, tends to be cast into the shadows, and your readers don't know what you believe or where your analysis is leading.

Let me also say something about plagiarism. Always be careful to give proper credit for all quotations and *any material not your own*, so as to avoid plagiarism. If you don't want to use the precise language of material from someone else, you can paraphrase, but you must mention who wrote it and the details of its publication. As a general rule, don't use more than three or four words in succession when paraphrasing. If your quote is four lines or more in length, indent this quoted material and type it in a smaller typeface, after identifying the writer and the publication details. In recent years, a number of famous writers and scholars have been found guilty of plagiarizing, so it is something that all writers—not just students—must be mindful to avoid.

Always carefully check your quoted material to make certain it is accurate and you have not introduced typing errors, left out words, or misquoted your source in any way. Our integrity as academics requires that we quote and paraphrase material correctly and always give credit to those whose material we are using.

Using Language Creatively—but Not Deceptively

There are endless ways to be creative with language. I've mentioned some earlier, such as humor and strategic repetition. Here, I'll touch on some examples of common rhetorical techniques—both ones to use and ones to avoid.

Metaphoric and Metonymic Writing

Metaphor is defined as a means of communication based on analogy. It is not confined to language, by any means, since print advertisements, television commercials, films, and many other kinds of texts in various media make use of metaphor.

In their book, *Metaphors We Live By*, George Lakoff and Mark Johnson explain the importance of metaphor:

> Metaphor is for most people a device of the poetic imagination and the rhetorical flourish—a matter of extraordinary rather than ordinary language. Moreover, metaphor is typically viewed as a characteristic of language alone, a matter of words rather than thought or action. For this reason, most people think they can get along perfectly well without metaphor. We have found, on the contrary, that metaphor is pervasive in everyday life, not just in language but in thought and action. Our ordinary conceptual system, in terms of which we both think and act, is fundamentally metaphoric in nature. The concepts that govern our thought are not just matters of the intellect. They also govern our everyday functioning, down to the most mundane details. Our concepts structure what we perceive, how we get around in the world, and how we relate to other people. Our conceptual system thus plays a central role in defining our everyday realities. If we are right in suggesting that our conceptual system is largely metaphorical, what we experience and what we do every day is very much a matter of metaphor.(3)

Metaphor, then, helps shape the way we perceive the world and the way we act in the world because, as the authors point out, our concepts govern our behavior.

A metaphor is based on a direct analogy and uses some form of the verb "to be," as in the example, "my love *is* a rose." There is a weaker form of metaphor, known as a *simile*, which uses "like" or "as." "My love is *like* a rose" is a simile. We use metaphors and similes to help us make sense of the world. If you are writing about something and can use a metaphor to help describe or explain it, you will be helping your readers by providing an orientation that will help them better understand what you've written.

For example, my first publication was in 1964 in Italy in a scholarly journal called *Il Mulino*. I was teaching at the University of Milan and did a research project on the Italian weekly press. I suggested that these weekly magazines were like dinosaurs: they had brains (their editorial staffs) that were the size of a pea and bodies (circulations) that were the size of dinosaurs. This analogy greatly amused many Italians and drew attention to the article; a news report about it was carried on an Italian radio station.

Metonymy communicates by association. As we grow up, we learn all kinds of associations, and thus metonymy can rely on these conventional associations to get ideas across. For example, we know that people who own Rolls Royce automobiles are rich, so when advertisers want to suggest an upscale product, they often use Rolls Royces or other expensive automobiles to make the connection. One might call it "gilt by association." Some examples of metonymy are: "I've got a BLT on table six" and "The pen is mightier than the sword."

A weaker form of metonymy is *synecdoche*. Synecdoche uses a part to stand for a whole (the Pentagon to stand for the U.S. military or the American flag to stand for the United States) or the opposite, a whole to stand for a part (America may win the next Olympics). We often use associations of one kind or another in our writing to put our readers in a certain frame of mind.

Avoiding Common Logical Fallacies

Academic writers should avoid common logical fallacies, such as selective inattention or "cherry picking" (neglecting data that would invalidate desired conclusions) and using experts with dubious qualifications and impartiality. Let's look at a few types of these errors in thinking.

Ad Hominem Arguments. Here the person is attacked rather than the argument. Usually this argument is used when one's position is hard to justify, so the opponent is attacked rather than the ideas.

Example: *We shouldn't elect Smith president, because he lacks the intelligence and vision for such an important position.*

Diverting Attention by Using Emotional Language. Here emotional language is used to justify a position rather than logic and evidence. This fallacy is generally used when one's position is weak.

Example: *Are we going to let those faceless bureaucrats in the United Nations, who live high on the hog on our tax money, tell us what to do about global warming? These global-warming fanatics are trying to scare the hell out of us, and we shouldn't let them get away with it!*

Begging the Question (*Petitio Principi*). Here the conclusion is assumed correct, which means the argument doesn't have to be supported. This is often done by assuming the answer to a question being discussed is so "obvious" it doesn't have to be defended.

Example: *Everyone knows that just a few bad apples in baseball took performance-enhancing drugs. We shouldn't let the bureaucrats who put together the report on them destroy the great game of baseball.*

Overgeneralizations. This is a very common mistake. Overgeneralizing means making sweeping claims that cannot be supported. If you write "all" or "every," be certain that you are not overgeneralizing. When in doubt, learn to qualify your statements.

Example: *Now we know that baseball players are all druggies. As the Mitchell report on drug abuse in baseball shows, by their use of performance-enhancing substances players have let down the American public.*

After This, Therefore Because of It (*Post hoc ergo propter hoc*). Just because X comes before Y, it doesn't mean that X causes Y. It is often difficult to determine what "causes" anything. So be very careful in asserting that one action or event caused another that happened later.

Example: *Every major war in which the United States has been involved has followed the election of a Democratic president. That's why it is correct to label Democrats as a "war party."*

Appeal to False Authorities. If you're going to use an authority, make sure the authority is legitimate. An authority on politics may not be an authority on education, so choose authorities with care. Also avoid ideologues or biased sources; make sure they're credible.

Example: *We shouldn't cut the defense budget. According to my physician, Dr. Jones, we should be spending much more on defense to protect America and the rest of the world.*

Incorrect Analogies. Be careful when making analogies because an incorrect, or false, analogy will weaken your argument. In earlier days, supporters of royalty suggested the following analogy, one that is hard to justify.

Example: *A country is like a human body, and it needs a king as the head.*

Misrepresenting the Ideas of Others. This is often a result of carelessness. If you quote an authority but leave out a word or phrase by mistake, you may alter the meaning of the material quoted. In other cases, writers select only the passages from quoted material that serve their purposes, which doesn't convey the original intent of the writer. See my earlier discussion of correct citations and avoiding plagiarism.

Example:

Mistaken quote: "We hold these truths to be evident that all men are equal."

Accurate quote: "We hold these truths to be self-evident, that all men are created equal."

Pushing Argument to Absurd Extremes. This involves things like ignoring qualifications people have made in their writings or in their reasoning.

Example: *Any attempt to legislate gun ownership will lead, inevitably, to the government taking away everyone's guns, which is intolerable and against the U.S. Constitution.*

When we write, we sometimes become so caught up in the documents we are working on that we neglect to be careful about our logic and the arguments we make. That's why taking some time away from a document we are working on is helpful; we can look at the text with a fresh mind and catch any overgeneralizations and other errors in thinking in time to correct them.

Now that you've learn something about style, I turn to a discussion of genres or kinds of academic writing, where you can use the rhetorical techniques and other tools I've covered in this first part of the book. Sometimes genres are described as "professional" writing—since people in professions often find themselves writing such documents. Because the part II of this book details the ingredients and parts of various kinds of academic texts, in some ways it resembles a cookbook or a set of instructions for assembling a piece of furniture. When you assemble a piece of furniture, or write a scholarly essay, you need the right tools on hand—and you need to know how to use those tools. You also need to know which tools are appropriate for each type of project.

PART II

GENRES OF ACADEMIC WRITING

Writing Effective Memos

M. JOURDAIN: I must commit a secret to you. I'm in love with a person of great quality, and I should be glad if you would help me write something to her in a short *billet-doux*, which I'll drop at her feet.
PHILOSOPHY-MASTER: Very well. . . . Is it verse that you would write to her?
M. JOURDAIN: No, no, none of your verse.
PHILOSOPHY-MASTER: You would have only prose?
M. JOURDAIN: No, I would neither have verse nor prose.
PHILOSOPHY-MASTER: It must be one or t'other.
M. JOURDAIN: Why so?
PHILOSOPHY-MASTER: Because, sir, there's nothing to express one's self by, but prose or verse.

—Molière, *The Bourgeois Gentleman*, Act II, Scene 6

News as Drama
When he was executive producer for nightly news programming at NJBJJC, Reuven Frank supposedly wrote the following memo:

Every news story should, without any sacrifice of probity or responsibility, display the attributes of fiction, or drama. It should have structure and conflict, problem and dénouement, rising action and falling action, a beginning, a middle, and an end. These are not only the essentials of drama; they are the essentials of narrative.

—Quoted in E. J. Epstein, *News from Nowhere*, 4–5

Professors spend a good deal of time attending committee meetings and writing memos, letters, reports, and proposals. It sometimes seems as though teaching is what professors do in spare moments when they aren't involved in endless meetings and occupied with writing memos and other such documents. Often we are like Benjamin Franklin in that prose writing—in this case writing in various academic genres—becomes the principal means of our advancement in the academic institutions where we teach. And for many of us, the ability to write these documents plays an important role in our careers more broadly and probably has as much as or more to do with our success than scholarly articles we write or books we publish.

Academic institutions are self-governing. The primary function of colleges and universities, generally, is to educate students and support professors who teach and research in various disciplines. Universities also provide myriad services to their students, from providing housing, health care, and parking places to maintaining libraries and laboratories. Universities are complex institutions, with thousands of students, faculty members, staff members, and administrators and require a great deal of work by faculty and administrators relating to all kinds of concerns. Faculty, for instance, serve on committees whose responsibilities include reforming departmental curricula or the general education curriculum to deciding upon new hires, weighing promotions, and granting tenure. These tasks require many meetings and streams of memos and letters.

Each of the genres of documents that we write in academic institutions has a specific format and task to perform. In part II of this book, I discuss the most important memos, letters, reports, proposals, and other academic genres and share my ideas about writing them more effectively. I will also present my ideas on the proper topics and how to format each of these documents. In many cases, I've used humorous and absurd examples of the various kinds of texts to liven up my discussions.

These documents are the means by which much of the decision making in academic institutions is facilitated and recorded. I begin with the workhorse of academic institutions: the memo.

Defining Memos

Memos are the most common form of written communication in academic institutions. For our purposes, a memo can be defined as *a short form of communication that is meant to be distributed internally in an organization or institution.* Often memos are written on prepared forms. Generally, they deal with one subject and are less than one page, although that is not always the case. Memos are rarely meant to be distributed externally—unlike the letters and, in some cases, reports and proposals that I'll cover in later chapters.

Sometimes faculty members have disputes with students, other colleagues, department chairs, and administrators. A common way that faculty members or administrators win these disputes is by showing, in memos, that their opponents didn't follow the procedures outlined in the faculty manual. That's why memos are so important. They are placed in personnel files and can be used in the event you are involved in a dispute and have to resort to filing complaints with grievance committees, arbitrators, and, if necessary, courts. Of course, most memos serve more mundane purposes and are meant to convey information of interest and importance to others.

Formatting Rules for Memos

Don't indent paragraphs; they should be flush left.
Single space each paragraph.
Place a line space between paragraphs.
Left justify your paragraphs.
Use charts and informational graphics to organize data.
Place a cc: and list the people to whom the memo is being distributed at the bottom of the memo.

A Sample Memo

As I mentioned, memos are generally written using specially designed forms or templates. But it is easy to create a memo on a computer that approximates the templates found in printed memo forms. The memo below shows a typical format for memos. It is short, direct, and detailed.

Date   November 12, 2010
To: Dean Miles Q. Gloriosus
From: Jane Doe
              Assistant Professor, Consciousness Studies Department
Subject: Meeting of November 11, 2010

Thank you for being kind enough to meet with me, and taking time from your incredibly busy schedule, to discuss my proposal for setting up a Center for Consciousness Studies.

I am gratified by your offer of $10,000 for equipment to help set up this center, which will play an important role in enhancing the university's

curriculum, the reputation of our department, the standing of our
school of psychology (which you so ably administer), and the image of
our university as a progressive and innovative one.

cc: Rasputin W. Tchitchikov
Chair, Consciousness Studies Department

Some memo formats also include a line drawn an inch or so under the
subject notation to separate the heading part of the memo from the written
text of the memo, but you can see the general format here. While memos, as
a rule, are short and direct, be certain that your memos contain all the relevant
information that the recipients of your memos need to know.

This memo does the following things:

- It records the fact that you met with the dean.
- It thanks the dean for spending his valuable time with you.
- It reminds him that he has promised you $10,000 for equipment.
- It asserts that this money will enhance the curriculum.
- It suggests the center will be good for the reputation of the university and, indirectly, for the dean.

Make sure you always save hard copies of your memos in case your computer crashes and you lose everything on your hard drive.

Typical Subjects for Memos

As I noted earlier, in the course of your career as a professor or administrator,
you will write many kinds of memos. Memos are useful, legally speaking,
because they are "paper trails" and offer a record of decisions made and actions
taken that can be used in the event of complications, controversies, and conflicts. Here are some of the most common types of memos.

Memos reporting on official decisions that have been reached. This kind of
memo reports on decisions that have been made by one or more members of
a university's administration or by members of some academic committee. The
memo describes a course of action to be taken. For example, it might be a
record of a department's decision about tenure for a faculty member or a dean's
statement supporting or opposing a promotion decision.

Memos reporting on understandings reached in conversations or in meetings.
These memos allow individuals or groups of faculty members to make sure that

certain events or decisions are recorded for possible future use. Professors should send a memo to department chairs or deans, after meeting with them, to record what was agreed upon.

Memos responding to a memo from someone else. You often need to reply to memos that you receive. In these response memos, you may explain an action you took, offer details and information about an action you plan to undertake, or amplify and clarify a previous memo. Faculty members often send a number of memos back and forth to one another about matters of mutual concern.

Memos recording minutes of meetings. Department meetings and committee meetings are often summarized in a memo that is distributed to all members of the department and, when relevant, to university administrators. Writing these memos requires discretion, for while it is necessary to be truthful, be careful about the way you characterize certain discussions and events that took place in a meeting. For instance, if the meeting has been contentious, focus instead on other things that happened in the meeting and avoid giving ammunition to anyone who may be hostile or who may want to do harm to one or more members of the department or to the department itself. What follows are two ways of describing what happened in a meeting.

Instead of writing:

An angry argument erupted at this point and members of the committee started screaming at one another. This was followed by a ferocious fistfight between the chair of the committee and the department chair.

write:

The discussion was lively and animated, with various positions affirmed by different members of the committee.

When you write memos about committee meetings, make sure you do the following:

- List the names of any administrators and faculty members and the department affiliations of all faculty members attending the meeting.
- List the topics that were discussed, summarize what was said about each topic, and record any decisions that were made and the vote count for each decision.
- Record any motions that were made, who made and seconded them, and the outcome of the voting on them, if the motions were put to a vote.

Cautions for Memo Writers

Remember that memos you write reflect your professionalism, can be collected in your personnel file, and, if a dispute or legal suit arises, can be used as evidence. So carefully word your memo. Never send a memo in haste and write anything that you may later regret having written. Here are some suggestions that may save you from embarrassment and grief.

Avoid insulting anyone, either directly or indirectly. Write in a formal, impersonal tone. Remember that in academic institutions some of the recipients have the power to affect your career, so be extremely cautious. The written word lives on, and it can be used against you.

Be judicious and circumspect. There are various ways of stating things ambiguously but which your reader will likely know how to interpret. Thus, you say one thing, which seems positive at face value, but your readers will know what you really mean. Consider the following examples of writing that might be found in memos involving tenure and promotion matters:

What We Write	What We Mean
John shows great promise	John hasn't done very much yet
Mary plays by the rules	Mary is inflexible and rigid
Jack's work is very practical	Jack's work has no theoretical value
Jane is an individualist	Jane isn't a team player
Bill is diligent and hard working	Bill isn't very smart
Betty is confident, self-assured	Betty has a monumental ego
George is determined	George will do anything to get ahead

We write using these code phrases so we can avoid receiving hostile memos by the people we are writing about if they discover what we wrote.

Never send a memo or any other kind of document in haste. I mentioned this earlier but it bears repeating. Sometimes we get upset and angry about an event (we weren't promoted, we were denied travel money, we didn't get the course schedule we wanted), and there's a tendency to assuage our feelings by sending a nasty or angry memo. Indignation always gets you in trouble, and words written in haste can have disastrous results. The same applies to e-mail, which I will discuss in chapter 12. I suggest you print out and reread any memos or e-mails that might cause problems; give yourself time to consider whether you really want to send an angry message that you may regret later.

Consider who will or may see your memo. Universities are bureaucratic institutions, so be mindful of following the proper chain of command and not going "over the heads" of others to whom you should have sent memos. For instance, don't antagonize a department chair or a dean by sending a memo directly to the president. Always consider how your memo will be distributed and who may read it. Send your memo to the person who can be the most helpful to you, but don't violate the chain-of-command rules for sending memos.

Ask colleagues in your departmental committees to review memos sent in a committee's name. If you're a member of a departmental committee, allow your colleagues to review the memo to make sure they agree with what you've written and to see if they have any suggestions. Let me offer a relevant example here. For a number of years, I was the chair of my department's promotion committee. One year, by chance, five associate professors were eligible for promotion to full professor, and our committee decided to support promotions for all five candidates. There were five members of the committee, so we each wrote one promotion memo. I asked each member of the committee to draft a promotion memo for one of the candidates, then the committee reviewed the drafts to make sure they made the best arguments possible. It is highly unusual for a department of around twenty professors to have five candidates for promotion to full professor, and it took a great deal of work on the committee's part to get the promotion memos in good shape. But through this process we crafted successful arguments, and all five of the professors were promoted.

Avoid sexist and other kinds of offensive language. As we read in chapter 4, it is now the custom to write in gender-neutral language. Avoid using singular male or female pronouns, using plurals instead. For instance, rather than writing "every professor has to learn how to deal with his or her problem students," write "all professors have to learn how to deal with their problem students."

Also avoid language that demeans a person or group based on race, religion, ethnicity, sexual orientation, or other characteristics. It is inappropriate to use offensive language in academic writing—or any kind of writing. As a result of the work of linguistic scholars and social scientists in various fields, we have become much more aware of the power of language and the role it plays in shaping feelings and identities.

We move next to academic letters, which, unlike memos, are often intended for external distribution. In my discussion of letters, I address the basic components of letters, the conventions for formatting letters, how to write effective letters, and the different kinds of letters academics are generally called upon to write.

The Art of the Academic Letter

My Illustrious Friend and Joy of My Liver!
The thing you ask of me is both difficult and useless. Although I have passed all my days in this place, I have neither counted the houses nor have I inquired into the number of the inhabitants; and as to what one person loads on his mules and the other stows away in the bottom of his ship, that is no business of mine. But, above all, as to the previous history of this city, God only knows the amount of dirt and confusions that the infidels may have eaten before the coming of the sword of Islam. It were unprofitable for us to inquire into it. O my soul! O my lamb! Seek not the things which concern thee not. Thou camest to us and we welcomed thee: go in peace.

> —Reply of a Turkish official to an Englishman's questions.
> Quoted in Austen H. J. Layard, *Discoveries in the Ruins of Nineveh and Babylon,* 663

Being entirely honest with oneself is a good exercise. Only one idea of general value has occurred to me. I have found love of the mother and jealousy of the father in my own case too, and now believe it to be a general phenomenon of early childhood, even if it does not always occur so early in children who have been made hysterics. . . . If that is the case, the gripping power of *Oedipus Rex,* in spite of all the rational objections to the inexorable fate that the story presupposes, becomes intelligible, and one can understand why later fate dramas were such failures. Our feelings rise against any arbitrary individual fate . . . but the Greek myth seizes on a compulsion which everyone recognizes because he has felt traces of it in himself. Every member of the audience was once a budding Oedipus in fantasy, and this dream-fulfillment played out in reality causes everyone to recoil in horror, with the full measure of repression which separates his infantile from his present state.

> —Sigmund Freud, letter to Wilhelm Fleiss, October 15, 1897

W e write letters to send information, to offer our ideas, and to argue for our beliefs and positions on issues. Like all writing, letters reflect our personalities and are often a valuable record of the times in which they were written. The letters of great political, historical, and literary figures are often collected and published because they tell us about the lives and times of these interesting people. These letters often have considerable literary merit, as well. In the age of the Internet and electronic mail, the art of letter writing seems to be fading away. This means we are now deprived of having a written record of our times. Fortunately, e-mails have not replaced academic letters, one area where letter writing is still practiced.

Defining Letters

I will understand an academic letter to *be a written document, in a traditional letter format, sent by university administrators, staff members, or faculty members to one another (internal letters) or to those outside of academic institutions (external letters).* We use memos for most internal communication inside academic institutions but in some cases we write letters—when we want to suggest a greater degree of importance or of personal interest.

In this chapter I will address the following:

- the basic components of letters
- typical letter formats
- how to write effective letters
- common kinds of letters you will be called upon to write

One type of letter, the "promotion letter," is technically a memo not a letter, but in most institutions it is frequently considered and referred to as a letter, so I will discuss it in this chapter.

Academic letters are generally written on university stationery and identify the administrative position or departmental affiliation of the writer. Let's first review the basic components of letters.

The Basic Components of Letters

Every letter writer has a different notion about the graphic design of letters, so it is possible to create and receive letters that don't look like the standard formats I discuss here. Generally, however, all letters have certain components.

Return address. The return address is included on university letterhead. If you are not using university stationery, provide a return address to direct any responses to your letter.

Basic Components of Academic Letters

Return address
Date
Inside address
Salutation
The body of the letter
The close of the letter
Signature
Additional information of interest

Date. Always give a date to establish when the letter was written. Usually it is aligned flush left.

Inside address. This provides the name of an individual or group to whom the letter is addressed. The inside address is usually included directly below the date and is aligned flush left.

Salutation. If the person to whom the letter is addressed has a doctorate or an administrative position, include this title in the salutation. If neither applies, use "Mr." or "Miss/Mrs./Ms.," as appropriate. When writing to a woman whose marital status you know, write "Miss" or "Mrs." If you do not know a woman's marital status or want to avoid the matter, write "Ms." Usually salutations are aligned flush left.

The body of the letter. Here you offer the information you wish to convey. You may state why you are writing the letter and what actions you would like the recipient to take. In academic letters, there are certain strategies to follow and common topics to include. You should do the following:

- State your conclusions before offering justifications and reasons for them.
- Make your requests before offering reasons for the requests.
- Answer any questions that may be of importance before offering explanations of your thinking.
- Discuss events of mutual interest.
- Offer data of interest.
- Refer to previous communications that have taken place.

By following these strategies and providing this information, it is possible for the reader to understand and follow your reasoning more easily.

The close of the letter. Usually a formal letter is closed with "Sincerely yours" or "Yours truly." Use a capital letter for the first word of a close.

Signature. In the signature line, include your name, your terminal degree, and your position in the administration or professorial rank. This material is usually typed four line spaces below your name (to leave room for your signature) and is aligned either flush left or flush with the signature. In the event a number of people have been involved in writing the letter, they should also sign.

Additional information of interest. In this section, below the signature, include enclosures ("enc.") and whether a copy of the letter is being sent to other people, in which case you name them ("cc: Provost James Joyce, Dean Rex Tyrannosaurus"). If the letter has been dictated, indicate this by including the initials of the letter composer and the initials of the person who typed the letter. For example, if I type a letter for Provost James Joyce, the notation would be "JJ:aab" or "JJ/aab."

Letter Formats

There are three commonly used formats in letters. Typically, letters are single-spaced with one line space between paragraphs. Because our eyes tire of reading long lines of typed material, leave substantial margins on the each side of the sheet of paper. Many writers leave an inch on each side, but I prefer to leave 1.5-inch margin on each side so the letter doesn't look crowded on the page.

Full block. In this format, every element of the letter is aligned flush left. This is considered to be the most modern format and is, I suggest, easiest to write and to read.

Regular block. This is similar to full block, except that the return address, close, and signature are moved to the right side of the letter.

Semiblock. This format is similar to regular block except that each paragraph is indented five spaces.

Deciding which format to use is a matter of personal choice. I prefer the full-block format with wide margins for my letters since I think it looks better and makes things easier for those who receive my letters. Let me show you a sample letter in this format.

Mind Publications   **Return address**
1234 Spinoza Street
Boston, MA 22222-3333

July 12, 2009   **Date written**

Dr. Immanuel Kant, Ph.D.   **Inside address**
Assistant Professor
Department of Cognitive Studies
Northwest Central Metropolis University
Metropolis, California 94949

Dear Prof. Kant: **Salutation**

We have received and evaluated your book manuscript,   **Body of letter**
tentatively titled *Critique of Pure Reason.* We
regret to inform you that although we find it quite
brilliant, we do not feel there is a suitable
market for your book. It is not suitable for
beginning philosophy courses or critical thinking
courses and therefore, because of the small number
of courses where it might be adopted, regretfully,
we will not be able to publish it.

We wish you good luck in publishing your book
and suggest you consider a university press or
other kind of publishing house.

We thank you for sending the manuscript to us
and giving us the opportunity to consider it.

Sincerely yours,   **Close**

                                                    Signature

Aristotle Plato
Acquisitions Editor

AP:soc   **Additional information**
cc: David Hume, Editor, Books Division

Common Kinds of Academic Letters

Two of the more common academic letters you will be asked to write are letters of recommendation for students and promotion letters. Let me suggest some topics for approaching these letters.

Letters of Recommendation for Students

You will be asked to write letters for students who hope to attend graduate school or are applying for jobs. These letters should contain the following information:

- What courses the student took with you
- Whether the student was an assistant of some kind
- How well the student performed in the courses
- Information on the character and intellectual abilities of the student
- Your predictions about the future success of the student

You should avoid mentioning anything about the student's race, religion, ethnicity, age, or other such matters.

Some institutions provide professors with letter templates that cover all the matters discussed above. In certain cases, it is useful to write a "To Whom It May Concern" kind of letter that deals with all scenarios in which the student may need a letter of recommendation.

Promotion Letters for Colleagues

We now move on to one of the most important kind of letters (for those involved) in academic institutions: the promotion letter. As I mentioned, even though this is commonly called a letter, it is generally an extended memo. The same kind of letter would be written for recommendations for tenure.

These letters should have the following components in varying degrees of detail:

- A statement about the promotion committee's decision to support (or not support) a candidate who is eligible for promotion (or tenure). When a decision is not unanimous, the number of positive and negative votes should be given.
- A list and evaluation of the candidate's publications, offering quotations from reviewers (when available) and assessments by members of the committee of the publications.

- A discussion of the candidate's service to the department and institution, listing service on departmental, school, and university committees.
- A discussion of the candidate's lectures and presentations at academic conferences and any positions held in academic organizations.
- An evaluation of the candidate's teaching abilities, with data from student evaluations and any relevant comments from colleagues.
- A discussion of the candidate's activities in the greater community.

Below is a sample promotion letter that covers most of these important points.

Date:	January 25, 2009
To:	Hieronymus Bosch
	Chair, Consciousness Studies Department
From:	Akaky Akakyovich
	Chair, Promotions Committee
	Consciousness Studies Department
Subject:	Promotion of Sigismund Freud to Full Professor

The Promotions Committee of the Consciousness Studies Department has voted unanimously to recommend that Associate Professor Sigismund Freud be promoted to Professor.

Professor Freud has published twenty-two articles in refereed journals on various aspects of his pioneering research on consciousness and its relation to the unconscious (see attached). He has also written two pioneering books on the unconscious, namely *Understanding the Dream* (Harvard University Press) and *Humor, Psyche & Society* (Oxford University Press) that have received favorable reviews. One reviewer said that Professor Freud's work has "brilliantly opened up the study of the unconscious for all to see." Reviews of his work are found in the Appendix.

We have also solicited letters on Professor Freud's behalf from a number of scholars at other institutions, such as Umberto Eco (University of Bologna), Jean-Baptiste Lacan (University of Paris), and Alfred Adler (Southwest Missouri State College).

In addition to his remarkable achievements in the field of research, Professor Freud has contributed in substantial ways to the department, the school of cognitive studies, and Central Northwest Metropolitan State College. He currently chairs the Hiring Committee and is a member of the all-university Curriculum Committee.

Professor Freud also has a superb teaching record. Over the past seven years he has had an average of 1.07 in student evaluations, with 1 being the most favorable and 5 being the least favorable on the scale. We are attaching all the student evaluations, along with letters from students who have studied with Dr. Freud and letters from colleagues in other departments who have worked with him on various committees. A peer evaluation by the dean of the college of cognitive studies described his teaching as "compelling" and "remarkable." (See attached in Appendix.)

The Promotion Committee believes, on the basis of the evidence submitted on Dr. Freud's behalf, that Associate Professor Freud merits promotion to Professor.

Academic institutions usually provide criteria for evaluating candidates for promotion or tenure, such as those listed above, and how the criteria are to be weighted. Given the careful scrutiny that a candidate will undergo, be honest and to mention a candidate's weaknesses as well as strengths, so as not to present an unbalanced and unrealistic picture of the candidate. Mention areas for improvement for a candidate and what the candidate is doing or can do to remedy them. Also detail the candidate's strengths and consider his or her areas of expertise. Be careful not to be too negative, however, lest you weaken your case. When writing promotion and tenure letters, keep in mind these suggestions for effective letters:

- Write in the active voice.
- Write directly and avoid qualifications.
- Inject as much detail in the letter as possible.
- Be mindful of the organization of the letter and keep related elements close to each other.
- Write clearly, avoiding awkward sentence constructions and jargon-filled passages.
- Be positive in stating your position.
- Write in the correct tone, since these letters are of great importance to the individuals being considered for promotion or tenure.
- Make certain that your letter doesn't commit any logical fallacies such as those discussed in chapter 5.

Remember that the quality of writing in your promotion letter has an enormous impact on everyone involved in the promotion process. You and your colleagues owe it to all candidates to make as strong a case as possible for (or against) promotion. Members of the administration will scrutinize every word you write, so the letter's style, its wording and polish, play a role in the decision making, especially for administrators.

Now we are ready to move on to the next topic: writing reports. Reports tend to be substantial documents and often include memos and letters of transmission within them. With effective report writing, you can demonstrate the quality of your thinking and your researching and writing skills. This will play an important role in your career.

Readable Reports

Just because people work for an institution they don't have to write like one. Institutions can be warmed up. Administrators and executives can be turned into human beings. Information can be imparted clearly and without pomposity. It's a question of remembering that readers identify with people, not with abstractions like "profitability," or with Latinate nouns like "utilization" and "implementation," or with inert constructions in which nobody can be visualized doing something ("prefeasability studies are in the paperwork stage.")

—William Zinsser, *On Writing Well,* 145–46

Even in a world such as we have today, in which everybody seems to be quarreling with everybody else, *we still to a surprising degree trust each other's reports.* We ask directions of total strangers when we are traveling. We follow directions on road signs without being suspicious of the people who put them up. We read books of information about science, mathematics, automotive engineering, travel, geography, the history of costume, and other such factual matters, and we usually assume that the author is doing his best to tell us as truly as he can what he knows. And we are safe in assuming so most of the time.

—S.I. Hayakawa, *Language in Thought and Action,* 33

M any of the most important decisions made in academic institutions are based on reports written by an administrator, faculty member, or—more often—a team of faculty members charged with investigating a topic and offering recommendations based on their findings.

Defining Reports

We can define a report as a *formal account that deals with the activities, proceedings, and conclusions of an individual or members of a group (often called a "task force") who have been charged with investigating a topic of interest and importance.*

Reports are meant to be objective, authoritative accounts of an investigation by the individual or group issuing the report, generally with a standard organization. In the material that follows, I list the basic elements of reports and discuss in some detail how to write them. The organization of a report may vary but most of the elements described below will be included.

Elements Found in Reports

The box below lists the elements typically found in reports.

Basic Elements Found in Academic Reports

Memo or letter of transmission
Cover
Title page
Preface or introduction
Table of contents
List of tables and illustrations
Acknowledgments
Executive summary
The body of the report
Recommendations
Appendixes
Bibliography and references

Let me include a bit more detail about each of these elements.

Memo or letter of transmission. This informs the readers of the report of the issue or matter being addressed. This memo or letter of transmission usually contains information about who commissioned the report and who wrote it. Thus, it contains the name of the individual or a list of members of the committee responsible for the report and the signatures of all involved in writing the report.

Cover. The cover usually includes the title of the report only.

Title page. The title page includes the title and the subtitle of the report (if there is one), the date completed, and the author or authors.

Preface or introduction. This serves to introduce the report to readers and may cover the reasons the report was commissioned.

Table of contents. The table of contents provides the readers with an overview of the report by listing the sections to be included. The contents should be written descriptively so readers will know what each section contains. Below I offer an example of the contents page from the Kaiser Family Foundation report "Food for Thought: Television Food Advertising to Children in the United States."

TABLE OF CONTENTS
EXECUTIVE SUMMARY
INTRODUCTION
NONPROGRAMMMING CONTENT ON TELEVISION—AN
    OVERVIEW
FOOD ADVERTISING ON TELEVISION
FROM THE CHILD'S PERSPECTIVE: ADVERTISING SEEN BY
    CHILDREN
CONCLUSION
METHODOLOGY
TABLES
REFERENCES

This report is available on the Internet at the Kaiser Family Foundation's website, listed in the bibliography of this book.

List of tables and illustrations. These lists provide data with the supporting evidence for the conclusions reached in the report.

Acknowledgments. Here the writers of the report thank anyone who provided information used in the report or was helpful in any way.

Executive summary. Most written reports (or other documents in educational institutions) provide conclusions at the beginning in the form of an executive summary. In the summary you offer evidence and arguments that lead to the conclusions reached. Think of the executive summary as a thesis statement, or a statement by a prosecutor or defense attorney at the beginning of a trial. Generally, executive summaries are short—no longer than one or two pages.

The body of the report. Here you address the typical questions that readers of the report may have, such as:

- Who is involved in the matter being investigated?
- Where did it take place or where is it taking place?
- When did it take place?
- What happened to merit a report?
- How did it happen?
- Why is the matter of interest and importance?
- How can the suggestions be implemented?

In answering these questions you will find that some of these questions demand longer treatment than others. Some reports, on relatively simple matters, are five or ten pages long; other reports, on complex and controversial issues, can reach a hundred pages or more. Readers tend to skim over long reports. But when personal interests or the fate of a program or department is involved, readers will scrutinize reports carefully.

Recommendations. Ultimately, reports lead to suggestions about a course of action to be undertaken or a policy to be implemented. These suggestions will be based on the factual material presented in your report. Make sure that the analysis and methodology of the report will hold up to the scrutiny of others.

Appendixes. This is where data and other material used in the report are offered.

Bibliography and references. Reports usually include a bibliography and references relevant to the matter being investigated.

Writing Reports

Here are a number of things to keep in mind when writing reports and, generally, all other documents in academic settings. Some of these suggestions have already been covered, but it is useful to review them in the context of reports.

Write in a formal, impersonal manner. Avoid writing in a style that suggests a lack of seriousness.

Avoid emotionally charged language. If you insult people, offer snide comments, and make emotional statements in your report, it will be seen as biased and invalid. Write in a reserved way; let your data and factual material make the argument for you.

Offer evidence that reasonable people would accept. Keep in mind that in reports dealing with disputes about curricula and other similar kinds of matters, both sides have reasons to support their positions. The side that "wins" is usually the one with the most compelling argument.

Offer detailed explanations of your decision making. Readers of reports are interested in knowing the factors involved in the thinking behind the report's conclusions. It is always a good idea to "show" and not just "tell" when writing. That is, demonstrate to your readers why you reached the conclusions you did, rather than asserting your correctness and asking readers to give you the benefit of the doubt.

Show why your conclusions are correct and opposing positions are incorrect. When writing a report about a topic that is controversial, or a matter of dispute, explain to your readers the negative and positive aspects of a proposed course of action. This is more effective than focusing on a single side of the issue.

Be focused and factual. A report should be based on fact-finding and objective, dispassionate research. Avoid conclusions that go beyond your data, which leave you open to attack or which are meaningless platitudes. Some elements you can use in writing your reports are:

- statistical data
- quotations from parties involved
- factual material
- testimony from experts

Be extremely careful in judging the truthfulness and veracity of information you are given by others who may be misinformed about the subject you are investigating. It is not easy to be objective and find out the facts in an investigation for reports. But you should try to present a truthful report and avoid being misled or lied to by those you are consulting for information, no matter the difficultly.

A great film by Akira Kurosawa, *Rashomon,* is a case in point. Something happens in a grove involving a bandit, a Samurai warrior, and his wife. The Samurai is killed, and his wife is raped by the bandit. A woodcutter, hidden in some trees, observes what happens in the grove from a distance. Yet, when the characters involved in the events in the grove are asked to offer testimony in a trial, each has a different account of the events. (The dead Samurai speaks through a medium.) This matter of different interpretations of an event offered by those involved or seeing has become known as the "Rashomon Effect."

Qualify questionable assertions. Be sure to qualify generalizations and assertions—since a single negative instance invalidates them. It pays to be cautious when making generalizations, but this doesn't mean you shouldn't come to a conclusion about the topic being investigated in your report. I make a distinction between a conclusion and a generalization here. Conclusions tell what the logical impact of an investigation suggests; assertions and generalizations cover large numbers of cases that are be related to what you've been investigating.

A Sample Report

Let me offer a sample report that contains many of the important report elements but in a concentrated or condensed version. I include a sample memo of transmission.

The table of contents describes what is in the report. The summary tells who (the president) charged the task force to make the report and what the mission of the report was. The body of the report describes how the task force looked for data and expertise from members of the faculty and others. The recommendation by the task force is described and the benefits from following its recommendation are spelled out. The summary of the findings reaffirms the decision reached by the task force and offers a timeframe for implementing its recommendations. In the appendix, a series of attachments is provided, including the names, ranks, and departmental affiliations of the members of the task force, letters pro and con from faculty members, descriptions of what is done at other institutions, and suggestions about what can be expected from setting up a teaching center.

Central Southwest California State University
1888 Main Street
Ragweed, California 94922

MEMO:
From: Myron Visigoth, Assistant Professor
    Chair, All-University Task Force on Teaching

To: Attila TheHun, Dean
Subject: Report of All-University Committee on Teaching

On behalf of the members of the All-University Task Force on Teaching, I am sending you a report with our findings for your consideration. It was a great honor for me to be asked to participate in the task force on this subject of such importance to the future of the university.

Table of Contents

Report from the All-University Task Force on Teaching

Executive Summary
At the request of Dean Attila TheHun, an all-university committee, "The Task Force on Teaching," was formed to investigate the value of setting up a center for the enhancement of teaching here at Central Southwest California State University. The Task Force solicited input from a variety of sources, including students, staff members, and faculty at CSCSU and invited experts from other institutions of higher education. As a result of our investigation, the members of the committee recommend, by a 9 to 4 majority, that a center for the enhancement of teaching be established here at CSCSU. A report from those dissenting from the majority opinion is included in the appendix of this report.

Activities of the Task Force on Teaching
The Task Force conducted weekly meetings and also met for a weekend retreat at the Alpine Lake conference center. Members of the Task Force also attended a number of national and international conferences on college teaching and submitted material based on the papers submitted and presentations offered at these conferences. The Task Force also invited a number of experts on college teaching to

give presentations and solicited letters from all interested parties on the proposed center. The Task Force formed several subcommittees to deal with such topics as designing the center, funding it, and finding the right person to direct it.

Recommendations
The Task Force recommends the following actions:

1. The center should be located in a central part of the campus where it will be easily accessible to students and faculty members.
2. It should have a full-time administrator, a secretary, and whatever technical staff is needed to run the center.
3. It should be seen as a resource for faculty members who wish to improve their teaching skills.

The Task Force recommends that the center be established by the beginning of the fall semester of 2010 and believes it will make an invaluable contribution to the quality of education at Central Southwest California State University

Appendix
The following materials are contained in this appendix: (1) the mission of the Task Force, (2) the members of the Task Force and their departmental affiliations, (3) a report on findings about teaching centers at other institutions of higher education, (4) dissenting opinions, if there are any, and (5) suggestions about operations at the proposed center.

Final Thoughts on Writing Reports

Although reports are written in a formal manner, they need not be written in a bureaucratic manner. Always make sure you write your report in an accessible style and use whatever rhetorical devices you can to make it as readable as possible.

Also, just as we saw in the discussion of when to use—or not use—humor, a good basic rule for academic writing is this: when in doubt, leave it out. In a report, if you have doubts about the veracity of any data or other information, it is prudent to avoid using it, since you want your argument to hold up to criticism. If you keep any questionable material, explain why you are using it and point out that there are doubts about its truthfulness. Sometimes this kind of material is useful in showing how the committee reached its conclusions. But take care to make your report as accurate as possible. Reports can be of considerable consequence for the institution where you are employed—and for your career there, as well.

Proposals are the "flip side" of reports. Reports are essentially investigations; proposals are designed to convince an individual or a group of people to take action. Proposal writing therefore demands an understanding of the complexities of human motivation.

Proposals That Persuade

A Modest Proposal.

FOR PREVENTING THE CHILDREN OF POOR PEOPLE IN IRELAND FROM BEING A BURDEN TO THEIR PARENTS OR COUNTRY, AND FOR MAKING THEM BENEFICIAL TO THE PUBLIC

I have been assured by a very knowing American of my acquaintance in London, that a young healthy child well nursed is at a year old a most delicious, nourishing, and wholesome food, whether stewed, roasted, baked, or boiled; and I make no doubt that it will equally serve in a fricassee or a ragout.

I do therefore humbly offer it to public consideration that of the hundred and twenty thousand children already computed, twenty thousand may be reserved for breed, whereof only one-fourth part to be males; which is more than we allow to sheep, black cattle or swine; and my reason is, that these children are seldom the fruits of marriage, a circumstance not much regarded by our savages, therefore one male will be sufficient to serve four females. That the remaining hundred thousand may, at a year old, be offered in the sale to the persons of quality and fortune through the kingdom; always advising the mother to let them suck plentifully in the last month, so as to render them plump and fat for a good table. A child will make two dishes at an entertainment for friends; and when the family dines alone, the fore or hind quarter will make a reasonable dish, and seasoned with a little pepper or salt will be very good boiled on the fourth day, especially in winter.

—Jonathan Swift, "A Modest Proposal"

W**e can define** proposals as *written statements that are meant to persuade someone (usually a department chair or member of the administration) to do something.* Implicit in a proposal is the notion that accepting it will be in the best interest of the institution. Proposals can be made by individuals or by groups. An infinite number of matters can be dealt with in proposals, such as requesting funds for travel to a conference, purchasing equipment, changing the design of a course, modifying the general education curriculum, or establishing a research center or laboratory. Desires (as reflected in proposals) are infinite, but the money to fund proposals is finite.

In a sense, proposals are similar to reports, except that the conclusions in reports are based, in theory at least, on fact-finding and objective research. In proposals, this is reversed—an individual or group starts with something they wish to be done and then support it with data and information. A course of action generally is implicit in reports, but not always. Let's look at the design of proposals and the means of making them credible—that is, the art of persuasion.

Basic Elements of Academic Proposals

Introduction
Body of text
Conclusion
Budget, when money is involved
Collection of documents supporting the proposal

Elements in a Proposal

There are many ways to organize proposals but they generally include the following elements:

Introduction. The introduction provides a general overview or contextual background of the situation that has led to the formulation of the proposal. It should be of interest to the readers of the proposal and suggest that the outcome of accepting the proposal will be of consequence.

Body of text. The body of text should supply the rationale for the proposal and discuss the benefits and value to be gained in accepting it. Proposals often include information on the qualifications of those writing the proposal and on how the proposal will be implemented.

Conclusion. The conclusion sums up the arguments made, discusses the importance of the proposal, describes the benefits of implementing the proposal, and suggests the proposal be accepted.

Budget, when money is involved. The budget shows how the money will be spent for those proposals that require funding. It is usually itemized to show, in detail, how money will be spent.

Collection of documents supporting the proposal. This documentation offers evidence that supports the body of the proposal. If, for example, your proposal involves changes in the general education program, the documentation might include statistics on student evaluations of the program, letters from students and faculty members interested in the program, and material on what other institutions have done, including the results obtained from changing their general education program.

A Sample Proposal

Note: Ordinarily a memo of transmission to the chair of the department would accompany this proposal; I have not included it here since I offered an example of a memo in chapter 8.

Proposal: New Course on Video Game Playing and Cognitive Learning

Introduction
Video games are now an important part of our popular culture, and the industry is now larger than the film industry. It is important to utilize the experience students have playing video games to enhance their educational experience.

Using Video Games to Facilitate Intellectual Development
This course, tentatively titled "Video Games, Psyche, and Society," would teach students how video games are constructed and use new video games that have been developed at various universities to explore their social and psychological impact. The course also would enhance their ability to think critically and to develop their research skills. I would use books such as Espen J. Aarseth's *Cybertext* and Janet H. Murray's *Hamlet on the Holodeck,* and articles describing research currently being conducted at a number of universities on video games

and education in America and in other countries. Part of the course would involve creating a virtual department in *Second Life*.

Conclusions
This course will put our department at the forefront of institutions using new media technologies for instructional purposes. I urge our curriculum committee to add this course to our department's course offerings.

The Art of Persuasive Writing

Rhetoric, Aristotle said, is the art of persuasion, and rhetorical techniques are methods writers use to make their arguments and convince their readers. It is a bit of a simplification to say that rhetoric always involves persuasion, but I say that because I want to caution writers against writing that leads nowhere (that is, to no conclusions), proves nothing, or fails to make a persuasive argument. Persuasion is critical to proposal writing.

Aristotle's views on rhetoric offer us some insights into the tasks that a writer faces. In the following passage from *The Basic Works of Aristotle*, Aristotle is writing about speech but we can substitute "written works" wherever he uses "speech" or "the spoken word":

Rhetoric may be defined as the faculty of observing in any given case the available means of persuasion. This is not a function of any other art. Every other art can instruct or persuade about its own particular subject-matter; for instance, medicine about what is healthy and unhealthy, geometry about the properties of magnitudes, arithmetic about numbers, and the same is true of the other arts and sciences. But rhetoric we look upon as the power of observing the means of persuasion on almost any subject presented to us; and that is why we say that, in its technical character, it is not concerned with any special or definite class of subjects. . . . Of the modes of persuasion furnished by the spoken word there are three kinds. The first kind depends on the personal character of the speaker; the second on putting the audience into a certain frame of mind; the third on the proof, or apparent proof, provided by the words of the speech itself. (1329)

According to Aristotle, speakers and writers use various rhetorical devices to persuade their audiences. In some cases, people who are recognized experts or authorities on a subject can persuade people, based on their reputations alone, but it is more effective to have what Aristotle called "proofs"—evidence that one's assertions are correct. But how do we persuade people to accept our ideas and assertions?

Basic Techniques of Persuasion

Below I list a number of techniques of persuasion that can be employed for your proposal. My focus here is on proposals involving needs to be addressed or problems and challenges faced by an institution, such as revising the general education curriculum or changing the requirements for graduation in a department.

Basic Techniques of Persuasion

Write in a confident tone.
Appeal to the decision maker's self-interest.
Tie your proposal to your decision maker's beliefs and values.
Focus on short-term or long-term benefits (or both).
Anticipate and refute possible objections to the proposal.
Show how your proposal is cost-effective.
Suggest that your proposal is the best of all possible solutions to the problem.
Show how other proposals that deal with a given problem are self-contradictory.
Appeal, in subtle ways, to your readers' emotions.

Write in a confident tone. If you write in a manner that suggests you assume the value of your proposal to be self-evident, it may help assuage any doubts that the colleagues or administrators who decide on your proposal may have.

Appeal to the decision maker's self-interest. Demonstrate that accepting your proposal is good for everyone concerned, due to the benefits that will occur if the proposal is accepted.

Tie your proposal to your decision maker's beliefs and values. This will enable you to strike a "responsive chord" and build your argument on the decision maker's beliefs, preconceptions, values, and attitudes.

Focus on short-term or long-term benefits (or both). Depending on the nature of your proposal, direct the decision maker's attention to either the short-term or long-term benefits—or both if you can—to be derived from accepting your proposal.

Anticipate and refute possible objections to the proposal. State possible objections to your proposal on your own terms so you can more easily refute them.

Show how your proposal is cost-effective. If you can show that the expense involved in funding the proposal will result in certain important benefits or in long-term savings, your proposal will gain wider acceptance.

Suggest that your proposal is the best of all possible solutions to the problem. There are often many different ways to solve problems, and you should argue that your proposal is better and more effective than others. One way to do this is to address the weaknesses of other proposals, as I explain below.

Show how other proposals that deal with a given problem are self-contradictory. Point out problems with other proposals, especially if they are inconsistent and self-contradictory. If you do this, you will gain more credibility.

Appeal, in subtle ways, to your readers' emotions. Focus attention on the benefits to your department, college, or university and the prestige to be gained, by all concerned, if a proposal is accepted. Point out how approving a proposal will help demonstrate that the decision maker is bold, imaginative, and a visionary.

Remember that proposals aren't always evaluated purely on the basic of logic and the validity of the arguments made in them. There is a human equation at work in evaluating proposals and making decisions about whether to accept or reject them, one based on factors such as friendships, moods, antipathies, grudges, and jealousies. These factors are at play in every aspect of university life, where, in principle, all decisions should be based on reason and logic alone.

Overcoming Resistance in Reluctant Decision Makers

Persuasion is the art of overcoming resistance and doubt in the minds of the target audience. Advertising is built on this principle, and a proposal can be viewed, without too much of a stretch of the imagination, as a kind of advertisement attempting to "sell" somebody on something

When writing a proposal, pay attention to the means of persuasion, listed above, which will help you to "sell" it to whomever it is addressed and to whomever might be reviewing it. You can't expect a positive response to every one of your proposals, but don't be discouraged. Advertisers don't convince everyone to purchase the products and services being advertised, and proposal writers can't expect to have all of their proposals accepted. But despite the problems caused by personality conflicts and other difficulties, a beautifully crafted and cleverly written proposal often convinces skeptical or hostile decision makers to adopt your idea.

Writing a Journal Article

The language game is similar to other games in that it is structured by rules, which speakers unconsciously learn simply by belonging to a particular speech community. Although players of the language game command a vast repertory of moves—that is a virtually infinite number of things they could possibly say in many grammatical combinations—nevertheless the number of possibilities is severely limited by the situation in which the speaker finds himself. . . . Unless he is a specialist in the subject of language, he is most likely unaware that he is following various complicated sets of rules which he has unconsciously acquired and internalized. Yet it is clear that he has incorporated such rules, for he recognizes speech that is "wrong"—that is, speech that departs from the rules—even though he does not consciously know the rules themselves.

—Peter Farb, *Word Play*, 6, 7

A basic structural design underlies every kind of writing. The writer will in part follow this design, in part deviate from it, according to his skill, his needs, and the unexpected events that accompany the act of composition. Writing, to be effective, must follow closely the thoughts of the writer, but not necessarily in the order in which those thoughts occur. This calls for a scheme in which those thoughts occur. In some cases, the best design is not design, as with a love letter, which is simply an outpouring, or with a casual essay, which is a ramble. But in most cases planning must be a deliberate prelude to writing. This first principle of composition, therefore, is to foresee or determine the shape of what is to come, and pursue that shape.

—William Strunk Jr. and E.B. White, *The Elements of Style*, 10

Getting an article accepted and published in a scholarly journal is probably the best way for scholars to enhance their chances for promotions, tenure decisions, and improved status among peers—even if only a relatively small number of professors teach at major research institutions where the "publish or perish" rule (and sometimes the "publish and perish" rule) applies. It usually takes about a year for a book to be published from the time it is accepted by a publisher, and it generally takes a year or two (or more) to write the book. So publishing a book is a long-term investment in time and energy. As a rule, it doesn't take as much time to write and publish journal articles, though the process still can take considerable time with some journals. It isn't unusual for an article that has been accepted by a scholarly journal to be published several years later.

Writing for Scholarly Journals

There are many kinds of scholarly journals. Some accept articles based on the judgment of their editors or their editorial boards, and many of the scholarly journals that function this way are of a high quality. But the more important journals, as far as academic prestige is concerned, are those that publish *refereed* or *peer-reviewed* articles, in which the editor sends an article, without revealing the author, to various experts in the appropriate field for evaluation. Generally, these peer reviewers are asked for their opinions on whether the article should be published as is, needs some work, needs a great deal of work, or shouldn't be published.

Among refereed journals there is a hierarchy . And some journals, often the preeminent journals in their fields, will publish only articles that they consider to be "paradigm changing"—that is, readers of the article, it is assumed, may change the way they think about the subject of the piece and the field itself. These journals tend to accept 10 or 15 percent of the articles that they receive, so it is difficult to get an article published in them. Some "A" level journals, such as the *Annals of Tourism Research,* are reputed to have a rejection rate of more than 90 percent. An article that is rejected by one of these prestigious publications may be a very fine piece of work and be readily accepted in other journals, so don't be discouraged if your work isn't accepted right away.

Consider submitting to journals in a variety of subject areas that might be covered in your article. For example, an article on the semiotics of tourism may possibly be of interest to journals in communication, sociology, psychology, economics, tourism, semiotics, or other disciplines or subdisciplines.

Planning and Writing Your Article

The first rule for writing scholarly articles is to make sure that you have written the kind of article that the journal publishes. Study the articles in the journal to get an idea of what topics are of most interest to the publication and examine how the articles are written. Make sure that someone else hasn't already covered your topic.

The second rule for writing scholarly articles is to carefully follow the journal's specifications for submitting articles. Often these specifications are found at the end of the journal or in websites maintained by the journal. In general, provide the following with your article submission:

- Title of article
- Abstract
- Intellectual questions addressed (sometimes called research questions)
- Literature review
- Hypothesis
- Research design and methodologies used
- Report on findings (the body of the article)
- Discussion of methodology and findings
- Conclusion
- References

What follows is material for submitting articles taken from the *Journal of Communication*, from a website maintained by the publisher, Blackwell. It is similar in nature to what you find with many journals and outlines what kinds of material the journal will publish.

The *Journal of Communication* is a general forum for communication scholarship and publishes articles and book reviews examining a broad range of issues in communication theory and research. *JoC* publishes the best available scholarship on all aspects of communication. All methods of scholarly inquiry into communication are welcome. Manuscripts published in *JoC* should advance knowledge about human communication. In addition, manuscripts should be methodologically sound, thoughtfully argued, and well crafted. Manuscripts must not have been published elsewhere or be currently under consideration for any other publication. Manuscripts are processed by blind review so author identification must be removed from all pages except the title page, which is retained by the editor.

If you were to write an article for this publication, be sure to follow its guidelines about style and content. Also, be certain that your article is on a subject of interest to the journal.

Let me call your attention to an excellent resource, available on the Internet and easily downloaded, by Barry Wellman, titled "Writing for International Refereed Journals" (see web address in the bibliography). Wellman's tips are appropriate for all journals but particularly pertinent to refereed ones. In writing articles for these journals, he suggests that there are a number of ways to improve your chances of having an article accepted.

- First, focus on communicating material of interest to others rather than displaying how brilliant and clever you are.
- Second, tell a "story," which involves organizing your material so that it proceeds logically and coherently and has a conclusion of interest. Your organization is of critical importance here.
- Third, avoid problems such as lack of focus, poor organization, gaps between your assertions and your evidence (evidence is not the same thing as illustrations or examples), and dated scholarship.
- Fourth, avoid jargon and endlessly citing "the usual suspects" such as Baudrillard, Barthes, Foucault, and Habermas, or others as appropriate to your discipline.

It is worthwhile to find Wellman's article on the Internet and to read it carefully. It considers many of the topics covered in this book, especially the matters of writing an interesting narrative and coming to a conclusion.

When you write a journal article, the entire text should lead to a conclusion that your readers will find interesting and useful. When you talk about your ideas and projects in conversation, you don't necessarily have to come to conclusions; you're not writing something for others to study and evaluate. But when you write in the expository mode, you must come to a conclusion about your topic—and you need to marshal the evidence and use the appropriate techniques of persuasion to support your conclusions. If you don't have anything to prove and therefore don't prove anything, your text will be formless and little more than meandering, conversational chit-chat.

Let me remind you of an important hint that I discussed earlier in the book: When you've finished writing your article, consider moving your conclusion to the beginning. Readers want to know what your conclusions are when they start reading the article. Articles are not mystery stories, so don't save the important stuff for the last page. Once you've told your readers your conclusions, you can then explain how you conducted your research and arrived at your findings.

Samples from an Article

In the material that follows, I offer a sampling from an article by Yaniv Poria and Yaniv Gvili that appeared in *The Journal of Hospitality & Leisure Marketing* in 2006.

Heritage Site Websites Content: The Need for Versatility

Yaniv Poria and Yaniv Gvili

ABSTRACT. This study examined the visitor expectations of a heritage site Website, a major marketing channel. The study focuses on Yad Vashem (The Holocaust Martyrs' and Heroes' Museum) in Jerusalem. The findings reveal the existence of three types of content that tourists expect to find on a Website: (1) functional information, (2) educational information, and (3) emotional information. Relationships were found between participants' perception of the destination relative to their own heritage, tourist motivations (overall and specific) to visit the destination, and tourist expectations of the Website content. The implications highlighted emphasize the attributes of the Internet as a communications channel that allows Website content to be tailored to the target audience and facilitate its use in marketing of heritage sites.

KEYWORDS. Customization, heritage, perception, motivation, Website.

This article contains the following elements:
    abstract
    keywords
    introduction
    literature review
    research objectives
    method
    findings
    conclusions (including management implications, limitations, and
        future research)

You can see from this selection how the article was structured and can discern, from the abstract, what the article dealt with and what its main findings were. The introduction addresses the impact of information technology on the tourism industry and discusses the theoretical and practical contributions of the study. The literature review mentions various scholarly studies that have been made of heritage tourism and the fact that relatively little work has been done on the use of websites as a marketing tool by heritage tourism entities. The research objectives section outlines the features of the study and two important aspects of the study: tourist perceptions of possible travel destinations and a consideration of the kinds of information sought by people when visiting websites. The method section explains why the authors chose Yad Vashem and how the authors use quantitative research methods in making their study. The findings section is the largest part of the article and has a number of tables detailing perceptions, motivations for visiting Yad Vashem, and kinds of information sought by people on websites. Authors typically discuss the limitations of their study and offer suggestions for future research on the subject in the conclusions section.

Formatting Your Article

When you write an article for a journal, be careful to use the proper format for that publication. Remember that different journals have different format requirements. For example, some want tables and charts shown in the article; others want them on separate pages. Here is the description of formatting required for articles sent to the *Journal of Communication*:

> **Manuscript Guidelines.** Prepare manuscripts in **strict accordance** with the fifth edition of the *Publication Manual of the American Psychological Association*. Submissions should usually not exceed 30 pages, including references, appendixes, endnotes, tables, and figures (keep endnotes to a minimum). The entire manuscript should be double spaced; standard type size (12-point) and standard margins are required; tables should be understandable independent of text. Manuscripts that do not follow these requirements or that are otherwise unsuitable for review will be returned to the author(s) without review.

This is a pretty standard formatting guide, but all journals differ in formatting and stylistic requirements. Let me offer an example of some material from an article on tourism.

This selection is from an article called "Living on the Edge," by Bob McKercher and Candace Fu, that appeared in a 2006 issue of the journal *Annals of Tourism Research,* generally considered to be the most important scholarly journal in its field. This journal requires authors to use numerous citations of tourism literature, and I have chosen an excerpt to point out the role of citations in articles written for this journal.

Much of the published material on tourism and the periphery has focused on Fringe destinations such as Pacific Islands, arctic regions, or rural communities (Brown and Hall 2000; Gets and Nilsoon 2003; Hall 1994; Pearce 2002; Prideaux 2002; Wanhill 1995; Weaver 1998). Only a few studies have examined the periphery of existing destinations. These have explored such themes as attributes-based approaches toward peripherality (Pearce 2002), residents' perceptions of the rural urban fringe (Weaver and Lawton 2001) and the periphery as a possible urban ecotourism venue (Dwyer and Edwards 2000).

Peripheral areas tend to be economically, socially, politically, psychologically, and developmentally isolated from and marginalized by the core (Botterill, Owen, Emmanuel, Foster, Gale, Nelson, and Selby 2002). They generally share a number of common features that accentuate their geographical disadvantages. They tend to have poorer infrastructure and services than the core; they are inaccessible, making communications difficult; their economic base is geared around primary production, which is now in decline; and what economic activity that does occur often has high leakages, as material must be sourced from the core (Botterill et al. 2002).

These citations, while they interrupt the flow of the article, are useful to scholars interested in the subject, as they provide important bibliographical sources. The citations also demonstrate the writers have done their homework and provide a defense against charges of plagiarizing ideas. Each journal uses a specific format, often borrowed from one of the major style guides—the Modern Language Association, American Psychological Association, and University of Chicago Press all have widely used style manuals. You should follow the one indicated for your journal.

Submitting (and Resubmitting) Your Work

As noted earlier, many journals may be interested in the topic you are investigating, and you should look at each of them to make sure your article covers a subject they consider important. Once you have composed a list of possible candidates for your article, send the editors of these journals a brief query describing your article to see whether the editor, or another appropriate person on the staff, wants to consider it for publication. If someone expresses interest, send the article but be prepared for long delays and possible rejection of the article.

In keeping with our *Journal of Communication* example, here is the guidelines section, which spells out the journal's submission and review processes:

Include a cover letter with author(s) address, telephone, e-mail address, and title of the manuscript. Submit three (3) copies of article manuscripts; attach abstract to each copy of the manuscript; do not identify author(s) except on the detachable title page. Also, provide an electronic version on disk in Microsoft Word. Submissions are NOT accepted by email attachment or fax (authors from outside of North America may request exceptions to this rule prior to submission).

Manuscripts meriting review will be read anonymously, usually by two referees. In most instances, authors can expect decisions on their work within 120 days. Because manuscripts receive expert review, and because the Editorial Board of *JoC* is international in scope, this time may vary. No manuscripts will be returned to authors. The *Journal* retains the right to make changes in accepted manuscripts that (in the opinion of the editor) do not substantially alter meaning as well as for grammatical, stylistic, and space considerations.

The *Journal of Communication* indicates that it can take as long as four months to process an article, which means do not expect quick results when you send in your work. The same holds true for many scholarly journals. As a rule, you cannot submit the same article to other journals at the same time (though some journals have relented on this matter). This means getting an article published in a scholarly journal can be a time-consuming and psychologically draining task. If you submit an article to a journal and it takes four months to come to a conclusion about whether to publish it, you've invested a great deal of time—in some cases close to six months, assuming you've spent two months writing it—in trying to get it published.

Sometimes, a journal editor will ask you to revise and resubmit your article; other times the editor will suggest specific changes for you to make. If either of these happens, it means you have a better chance of having your article accepted. I dealt with this process of writing and revising your work earlier, and you may wish to reread this material. Make sure you don't let this opportunity to publish an article slip away from you by not adequately revising your material.

In other cases, however, the editor of the journal may reject your article for a variety of reasons. Your article may be rejected because the editorial staff doesn't agree with your research methodology, doesn't think your findings are of consequence, doesn't consider your topic important, or already has published something in the same area of research. Remember not to take the rejection personally and become discouraged. Although I've published a considerable number of articles and books, I've received countless rejection slips and letters over the course of my career. I never let them bother me. Keep plugging away and assume that some editor, somewhere, might want to publish your article.

Reviewing Books for Journals

Writing book reviews for the book review sections of many scholarly journals is another possibility—and this is an easier process than submitting scholarly articles. You can arrange to write book reviews by contacting the book review editor and offering your services. Be sure to indicate your areas of expertise. Publishing a book review isn't as prestigious as publishing an article, but a publication of any kind is still a feather in your cap. If you are interested in writing reviews, study some reviews published in the journal to get an idea of their length and content.

When reviewing a book, offer your readers an overview of the book and an analysis of its strong and weak points, offering evidence to support your contentions. Then offer a final verdict on the importance of the book to scholars in the field. Some book reviewers can be nasty and write hostile and insulting reviews. A reviewer of one of my books on television concluded his review with, "Berger is to the study of television what Idi Amin is to tourism in Uganda." He was not sympathetic to my psychoanalytic and semiotic interpretation of various television programs. Another started his review of one of my books by writing, "How do you review a book that should never have been published?" Writing this kind of a review is not a service to your readers or yourself, so if you get the chance to review a book, focus your energy on the book's content and discussing its value to those in the field.

Writing for Nonacademic Publications

Many popular magazines accept essays in which scholars use their expertise to approach some topic of general interest. Before writing articles for these publications, just as with scholarly journals, carefully study them to understand what writing style to adopt. Usually these articles are written in an accessible style, designed to "hook" readers at the beginning of the piece and to end with a "punchy" conclusion. It also helps to have a clever title. You should always query editors first to see whether they are interested in considering your article and to explain the argument you will be making.

In addition to writing books and articles for scholarly journals, in the course of my career I have written freelance articles in newspapers and magazines such as the *San Francisco Chronicle,* the *Los Angeles Times,* and *Rolling Stone* on various aspects of popular culture, media, and humor. What you will find when you do such freelance writing is that editors are interested in articles that will appeal to their readers. Once an article is accepted, you may be able to develop a working relationship with the editor and place other articles in that publication.

Because of the financial squeeze many newspapers are experiencing, they have curtailed the amount of freelance material they accept in recent years. But some opportunities with newspapers still exist, and magazines are always looking for good material. Whatever the publication, make sure your writing is entertaining and informative—offering your readers insights into subjects that they will find interesting. You can find magazines that may be interested in your work at any decent bookstore; they are listed in publications such as *Writer's Market* and other magazines devoted to writing.

Whatever reasons editors may give for rejecting your article, they should never reject your article because it is poorly written. That matter is completely under your control, and if your article is beautifully written, it gives you a leg up. Sometimes well-written articles with weak arguments and unsurprising findings get published and awkwardly written articles with important findings don't get published.

Aaron Wildavsky was, before his untimely death, a world-famous political scientist. He had been dean of the School of Public Policy at the University of California, Berkeley, and was elected the president of the American Political Science Association. His articles were rejected from time to time—not because his work wasn't worth publishing, but because an editor deemed it unsuitable for the particular publication that rejected him.

"When I get an article rejected," he once told me, "I take it out of the envelope from the publication that rejected it and put it in another envelope and send it off, the next day, to a different publication."

So if you get rejected, don't despair. Just like Aaron Wildavsky, you should put your article in a new envelope the next day and send it to another publication. And then you should speculate in your own journal about other topics you wish to investigate and other articles you might want to write.

Writing an Academic Book

Everything in life has to start somewhere and that somewhere is always at the beginning. The same is true for writers. Stephen King, J. K. Rowling, John Grisham, Nora Roberts—they all had to start at the beginning. It would great to say that becoming a writer is as easy as waving a magic wand over your manuscript and "Poof!" you're a published writer, but that's not how it happens. There's no magic potion or one true "key" to a successful writing career. However, a long, successful, well-paid writing career *can* happen when you combine four elements:

- Good writing
- Knowledge of writing markets (magazines and book publishers)
- Professionalism
- Persistence

Good writing is useless if you don't know which market will buy your work or how to pitch and sell your writing. If you aren't professional and persistent in your contact with editors, your writing is just that— *your* writing. But if you are a writer who possesses, and can manipulate the above four elements, then you have a good chance of becoming a paid, published writer who will reap the benefits of a long and successful career.

> —Kathryn S. Brogan, "Getting Published: Before Your First Sale," *2004: Writer's Market*

If you think about it, a book is a collection of chapters, each of which can be thought of as similar to an article generally of fifteen to thirty pages, except that articles stand alone and chapters are part of a larger topic that is being written about. If you've written fifteen articles, each around twenty pages in length, you've written the page equivalent of a book. And many books are little more than a collection of articles or essays.

Deciding Which Kind of Book to Write

As a rule, writers don't just sit down at the computer and write a book off the top of their heads. A writer must decide what *topic* to write about and what *kind* of book to write. As an academic writer, you would likely choose one of three options: a professional book, a scholarly research book or monograph, or a textbook. You may also want to edit a book of collected articles by various writers and group them into themed parts or sections. Publishers tend to be wary of edited books, but if you can find important articles and make your edited book "flow" (inject some continuity into it), you can come up with a valuable book that might sell well. What follows are brief descriptions of the most common books written by academics. The distinctions I've made among these three categories are somewhat arbitrary, of course.

Professional books. Professional books are written by scholars on topics of interest to other scholars in the field. Sometimes they are written for the general public or occasionally as texts or supplementary texts in courses. Many professors don't assign large textbooks but ask students to read a number of shorter professional books. In recent years, professional books have changed to look more and more like textbooks, though generally they aren't as comprehensive as textbooks. I always thought of myself as a writer of professional books, but over the years, as editors have asked for study questions, games and activities, and other apparatus, my professional books have become close to being textbooks.

Textbooks. Textbooks are overviews of classroom subjects and are usually accompanied by a considerable amount of apparatus: study questions, bibliographies, and teaching aids. Many textbooks are written by teams of scholars with expertise in the subject matter of the book. A textbook is usually long and comprehensive—to cover an important topic of study and to be the main text in a course.

Some textbooks are readers—edited works or anthologies with articles by scholars as part of a general collection on the subject being covered. It may seem as if creating an edited work is easier than writing a book, but an enormous amount of work is involved in finding the right articles and in obtaining permission to use them. Sometimes a good deal of expense is tied to securing these permissions as well. If some of the articles are written as original pieces for your reader, you may need to badger your contributors to finish their chapters, to revise them, and to turn them in on time. You are also expected to provide commentary on the articles and may find yourself writing much more for your edited text than you thought you would.

Scholarly books or monographs. These types of books are designed to investigate in depth specific topics of interest to the writers, without any consideration for possible use in college and university courses. Some scholarly monographs, however, are used in courses, though these monographs have no apparatus.

In an earlier chapter, I discussed the importance of writing for a target audience. Your decision about your target audience will affect your choice of topic, what kind of a book to write, and the writing style you adopt. Be sure to factor in a number of considerations: Who might be interested in this topic or some aspect of it? What is the best way to write a book that will appeal to them? How can I make the book as accessible and interesting as possible?

Write the Book before the Query!

Let's say you are interested in a topic and you want to write a book about it. First be sure your topic can sustain a book-length treatment. Then you will face a dilemma: "Should I write my book without a contract from a publisher, or should I send off queries and prepare a proposal and some sample chapters to send to any editors who might be interested in the projected book?" On the one hand, you want to write the book because you are interested in investigating the subject and feel confident it will find a publisher. On the other hand, you don't take chances and want to secure a publisher interested in your project before you begin.

My advice is to take the first course of action: Write the book! But to do so, you should have confidence in your abilities and feel that eventually you'll find a publisher. This may seem unusual advice. Most professors are unwilling to take a chance on writing books that may not be published and so adopt the second course of action: Find a publisher first. But there are problems with this approach. For one, it may take a long time before you find a publisher for your book. Certainly, while you are waiting you can write articles. But the passion for writing the book you want to write will probably fade over time. Then, when you finally do get the go-ahead from an editor, you likely won't be in the same mood and won't be as excited about the book. In addition, just because you have a contract for a book proposal doesn't mean the editor will accept the written manuscript. So, it may take you a year or two (and in some cases much longer) to get a contract and write your book, and it still may not get published. This doesn't happen often, but it is something to think about. There is one other thing to keep in mind here: your book proposal will require a sample chapter or two. My suggestion is this: As long as you've written sample chapters, continue writing and finish the book.

When I find a subject I want to write about, I go ahead and write it, even though I can't be sure it will be published. And, I must admit, I have written some books that weren't published. This means I "lost" the time it took to write the book. But what I gained was learning more about the subject, practicing my craft as a writer, and in some cases, writing material I could use in a different book. Baseball players don't expect to bat 1.000 and neither should academic writers. If worse comes to worst, you can self-publish your book at little or no cost. At the end of this chapter, I'll suggest a few ways to publish your own books.

Writing Queries That Will Interest Editors

A query is a short letter sent to editors that describes in general terms the book you plan to write or have already written. It should say something about your educational background and the courses you teach. You should also discuss the audience for your book, what courses your book will be used in (if applicable), and what is distinctive about the book. Mention that you have prepared a proposal, should the editor wish to obtain more information about your proposed book. Below I offer an actual query I wrote for *Making Sense of Media.* Although I am not including the letter that went with it, you should include a brief cover letter as well. Your letter should also say something about your education, background, and areas of expertise, if this material isn't in your query.

Rationale
This book will explain in an accessible manner a number of ideas and concepts that will help readers make sense of media. These ideas are taken from what I (and most others who write about the media) consider to be seminal, canonical, classic or "key" texts that critics and scholars of all persuasions use in analyzing media. I have, so to speak, rounded up "the usual suspects" (Barthes, McLuhan, Bakhtin, Eco, etc. etc.) and will discuss one of their books that I feel has material of interest and utility to readers. In each case, I will select books to deal

with that contain material that I consider to be essential for readers interested in understanding and interpreting media. I have also chosen works that allow me to deal with certain topics that I consider to be important. The purpose is to provide readers with a repertoire of ideas and concepts that they can call upon when dealing with media and mass mediated texts. Since the media transmit texts, my focus will be on texts that media carry rather than just talking about the media in general.

Competition

There are an enormous number of books that deal with the media from every perspective one might think of. There are readers full of articles on the media. There are dictionaries of key concepts. There are books with analyses made from different disciplinary and ideological points of view. But there are few books that I know of that deal with the media in terms of what might be called the "key texts" that form the foundation for most of the media criticism and analysis. My book will be similar in design to Lowery and De Fleur's *Milestones in Mass Communication Research: Media Effects,* which focuses upon important studies in media communication research, and Katz, et al's *Canonic Texts in Media Research,* but my book will deal with media, in general, and will be written for readers who have no prior knowledge of media theories and analytical techniques. My goal, then, is to provide students with a familiarity with some seminal works and some of the most important concepts in these works that they can use in making sense of the media.

Design of the Book

As I envision the book, it would consist of a number of relatively short chapters (eight to ten pages), each of which would be devoted to some of the more important ideas found in a book. There would be a quotation either about the author or the book or from the book to start off each chapter. Then I would discuss and explain a few of the ideas found in the book that I think are most interesting. I would make liberal use of quotations to show the style of the authors and the way they stated their ideas and, in some cases, relevant quotations from other authors as well. I should add that my theory of teaching is to give readers ideas, concepts, methods, insights, and the like that will enable them to make their own analyses of media rather than offering articles that do this for them. The "reader" as I see things should be the person who learns ideas and concepts not a book full of articles by other "readers."

Market

The book will be written in an accessible style and is designed for lower division students taking introductory courses in media studies, communications, popular culture, cultural studies, and related areas. Titles for such courses might be "An Introduction to Mass Media," "Analyzing Popular Culture," "Media and Society," and "Media and American Culture." Because of the way it will be written, my book can also be marketed as a trade paperback.

It is possible to use the Internet to e-mail queries to editors and that practice is acceptable to many of them, but I suggest you use snail mail to save the editor the bother of printing out your query. The easier you make things for editors, the better your chances will be.

The problem editors face with queries is that while many professors have ideas about books they want to write, they often don't have the time or discipline to write the books—or, in some cases, what they write isn't publishable. So editors are always in a bind, especially when it comes to professors who have not previously published books. Editors often reject books that go on to sell huge numbers of copies and accept books that they think will be best sellers but don't sell well at all. Every book published represents a considerable outlay of money by the publisher. If publishers don't consistently sell enough books to cover their expenses, they go out of business.

If you've had an expression of interest in your query, your next step is important—submitting a proposal.

Writing a Convincing Book Proposal

After you've received a positive reply from an acquisition editor, your next task is to write a proposal that will be convincing and lead to a contract. The editor will probably send this proposal to other scholars in your field to evaluate, so be sure your proposal is as well written as it can be. Research your publisher's submission guidelines to make sure you are following them.

When you send a book proposal to editors, they generally want to see the following:

Description of the book. Here you will describe the book again, in a manner similar to your query, and provide the editor with an estimate of how many words and pages your final book manuscript will be. Your editor will probably send your query to some professors in the field, who will not have seen your initial inquiry, so remember to offer a fairly complete description of your book.

Main Components of a Book Proposal

Description of the book
Table of contents
One or more sample chapters
Sample of the teaching apparatus to be used (if applicable)
Comparison of your book with competing books and description of
    intended audience
Schedule for completion of book manuscript
Vita

Table of contents. The contents is provided so editors can get an idea of what topics will be covered in the book. List your chapters and indicate in some detail what they will deal with.

One or more sample chapters. Provide several sample chapters so editors can see how well you write.

Teaching apparatus. The teaching apparatus that will accompany or be part of your book, if applicable, includes elements such as learning games and exercises, study questions, and topics for research papers.

Comparison. Provide a comparison of your book with competing books, and the reasons why your book is superior to the others. If there is a leading text in the same area covered by your book, discuss that text in some detail and suggest how your book will be better. Also include a description of your intended audience and the size of the market for the book.

A schedule for completion of book manuscript. You should be explicit to your editor about when you expect to submit a first draft, how much time will be needed to revise your manuscript, and the date when you anticipate submitting a final draft. If you have already written the book, you need only consider the time needed for revisions, as suggested by your editors or the professors reading the proposal.

Vita. Submit a vita describing your educational and professional background, the courses you've taught, any articles you've published, and anything else that will give editors confidence in your knowledge of the subject and ability to write the book.

These are reasonable subjects for editors to be curious about, and you should do whatever is necessary to convince them that your book merits publishing. As a rule, academic publishing doesn't make use of literary agents, so you function as your own agent. As noted earlier, visit the websites of the publishers to whom you send your proposals to see if they have any submission guidelines; to learn whether they accept unsolicited proposals; and to determine whether they want them by e-mail or require hard-copy proposals.

A Sample from a Book Proposal

Here is a portion from my proposal for my book, *Making Sense of Media: Key Texts in Media and Cultural Studies.* I offered a query from the proposal earlier. In this selection, I list the authors and texts I consider using. When I wrote the book, I selected nineteen texts, some of which were not in my original listing of authors, books, and topics.

Prospectus

(Tentative Title and Table of Contents)
Making Sense of Media
Key Texts in Media Analysis and Cultural Criticism

Author	Book	Topic
Aristotle	*Poetics*	Narratives
Bakhtin, Mikhail	*Rabelais and His World*	Dialogism, carnivalization
Barthes, Roland	*Mythologies*	Applied semiotics
Benjamin, Walter	"The Work of Art in the Age of Mechanical Reproduction"	Auras
Berger, John	*Ways of Seeing*	Visual aesthetics
Cantril, Hadley	*The Invasion from Mars*	Research, mass behavior
Certeau, Michel de	*The Practice of Everyday Life*	Resistance, pop culture
Eco, Umberto	*The Role of the Reader*	Reader/writer relationship

Eisenstein, Sergei	*Film Form*	Montage
Freud, Sigmund	*Jokes*	Humor
Goffman, Erving	*Gender Advertisements*	Advertising, images of women
Haug, Wolfgang	*Critique of Commodity Aesthetics*	Esthetics of consumption
Jameson, Fredric	*The Prison-House of Language*	Structuralism
Lakoff & Johnson	*Metaphors We Live By*	Metaphor, metonymy
Lefebvre, Henri	*Everyday Life in Modern World*	Advertising, everyday life
Lyotard, Jean-François	*The Postmodern Condition: A Report on Knowledge*	Postmodernism
Lotman, Yuri	*Semiotics of Cinema*	Semiotics, cinema
McLuhan, Marshall	*Understanding Media*	Hot/cold media, print
Murray, Janet	*Hamlet on the Holodeck*	Video games, holodecks, etc.
Noelle-Neuman, Eliz.	"The Spiral of Silence"	Spiral of Silence, public opinion
Propp, Vladimir	*Morphology of the Folktale*	Narrative theory
Saussure, Ferdinand de	*Course in General Linguistics*	Semiotics
Sontag, Susan	*Against Interpretation*	Formulas
Wildavsky, Aaron	"Choosing Preferences by Constructing Institutions: A Cultural Theory of Preference Formation."	Political cultures
Williams, Raymond	*Marxism and Literature*	Marxism and media

Introduction: The Media in Our Lives
We spend an incredible amount of time using media. From the moment we get up in the morning until the time we go to bed in the

evening, we listen to the radio, watch television, play video games, play CDs, send e-mail to our friends, and read newspapers, magazines, and books. The statistics on media use are simply incredible. If you are a typical American, you spend:

around four hours a day watching television

around one hour a day listening to the radio and CDs

around one hour a day reading books, newspapers, and magazines

to which we must add time for all the other activities that involve media. Children spend around forty hours a week involved with media or one kind or another—that is, the equivalent of a full workweek with the media.

We may ask ourselves, "So what? What difference does it make?" My answer is that all of us who use the media should be more aware of what the media might be doing to us. We use the media for our own purposes but we must be aware of how the media use us! The media help shape our social institutions, our political order, and our culture, which means the media, directly and indirectly, play an important role in socializing and acculturating us.

Let me offer an insight from the French sociologist Emile Durkheim. Durkheim pointed out that there is a dual process that goes on as far as individuals and society are concerned. We are in society and, though we may not be aware of this all the time, society is in us. By this he meant that as we grow up in a society, we learn certain values, beliefs, and practices that affect us in profound ways.

Defining Media

A *medium* can be defined as a means of sending or communicating messages, information, or texts of one kind or another, from one person to another or, in the case of the mass media, to many people. In academic discourse, the term "text" is used to mean any work of art—a radio or television commercial, a television show, a film, a song, whatever. *Media* is the plural of the term medium. Media communicate texts. For example, speech is a medium we use in conversations with one another; it is a personal medium. The mass media are generally held to include books and other kinds of printed works, radio, film, television, CDs, DVDs, and the Internet. With the mass media, large numbers of people are involved as audiences in the communication process.

There are many different ways of classifying media. Some scholars classify media according to whether they are electronic or print media. Others make a place for visual media. However you wish to classify media, there is no doubt that we spend a great deal of time, every day, using media—and, some would say, allowing media to use us!

Consider the following: approximately 70 percent of newspapers and magazine space is devoted to advertising, and radio and television devote an enormous amount of time—sometimes as much as a third of an hour—to playing commercials. The average situation comedy lasts twenty-two minutes; the remaining eight minutes is for commercials. As many commentators have pointed out, the purpose of television shows—as far as advertisers are concerned—is to deliver audiences to advertisers. The obsession radio and television stations have with obtaining money from advertising helps shape programming.

One question that has dominated the work of scholars involved with studying the media is—how do the media effect our families, our friends, our societies, and us? Do the media flow off our backs like water off the backs of ducks—that is, are the effects of our exposure to the media short lasting and trivial, or do the media have profound and lasting effects upon us—effects that we may not necessarily recognize but which, nevertheless, may shape our ideas and behavior in important ways?

Key Texts in Media Analysis and Cultural Studies

Over the years, philosophers, linguists, psychologists, sociologists, and communication scholars have written important articles and books that deal with the media. What I offer in this primer are a number of what I call "key texts"—works by writers and scholars that offer important insights into how the media work and what their effects upon us might be. I discuss a number of interesting ideas from important books in media analysis and cultural studies (since media is so much a part of our culture) which will help you decide whether or not the media have effects that are powerful and long lasting or weak and of no great concern. And what those effects might be.

Important Concepts

I do not deal with every idea in each book—that would require an enormously long book. There are books, listed in the bibliography, on many of the authors I deal with that you can consult if you wish a more detailed look at their ideas. Instead, I offer some important ideas that will help you make up your minds about the role of media in your life and in society, politics, and culture. I offer a number of quotations from these key texts so you can see how the authors explained their ideas.

I have written this book in a manner so as to make it accessible to the average reader and thus I have avoided, as much as possible, using the jargon that many academic scholars use in writing about media and culture. This jargon is often found in scholarly journals and is understood by the people who write articles in these journals and who read the journals. But it is inappropriate to use this jargon very often in a book designed for the general reader.

Since media is so much a part of our lives, learning about the media is indirectly a way or learning about ourselves—about where we got our ideas about what is important in life, about what we should expect out of life and about how we should behave. Most people believe that their experiences play an important part in their lives; a chance remark can have incredible consequences (as the former leader of the Senate, Trent Lott discovered). If that's the case, shouldn't mediated experiences count for something? That question is something you might keep in the back of your mind as you explore this fascinating and important subject—and learn how to make sense of the media.

I should add that my proposal was accepted and I was offered a contract for the book. When I sent in the manuscript, my editor wrote me a positive note: "It is everything that I could have expected."

Formatting Your Manuscript

Now, let's assume that your proposal has been accepted and you are writing the first draft of your manuscript—keeping in mind the hints and suggestions I offered in my earlier chapters on topics such as formatting, style, persuasive writing, and meeting deadlines. Your editor may provide you with specific guidelines for formatting your manuscript. If not, let's review some general tips. Earlier I suggested that you adopt a format with wide margins and not too many words on a line, since the eye gets tired reading long lines of typewritten material. For example, I use 1.85-inch left and right margins, giving me ten to fifteen words on a line, which is easy on the eyes of the reader and enables me to do a good deal of revising in the margins of my manuscript once I've printed it out. A few other recommendations and reminders include:

- Left justify your manuscript's margins. Do not justify margins on the right (or use full justify), since doing so leads to gaps between words that make reading difficult.

- Write in 11- or 12-point Times Roman or a similar easy-to-read typeface. Avoid sans serif fonts, since they are harder to read, and avoid using a number of different typefaces, since this gives your manuscript a gimmicky look.
- Double-space everything, including excerpts, notes, and references.
- Avoid writing any text in all caps, since it is difficult to read.
- Use white space to draw your reader's eyes to important material. White space makes material readable, not the size of the typeface used.
- Use lists, charts, and graphs to organize material.

Always remember to proofread your manuscript to eliminate typing errors (typos) and to check that your citations and quotations are correct, your bibliography is complete, and the desired documentation style is consistent.

Handling Rejection without Depression

Writers live to write books and editors live to reject them. The important thing is not to become depressed about being rejected or about having things fall apart when dealing with a publishing house. Just as you do when you send an article off to a publication, when you send a book or proposal to a publisher, always have a list of other places to submit your manuscript if it is rejected. I suggested this in the previous chapter, sharing the advice of scholar and author Aaron Wildavsky, but I want to emphasize again how important it is.

In 1981 I wrote a book on methods for analyzing media. The first part of the book was about semiotics, Marxist theory, psychoanalytic theory, and sociological theory. In the second part of the book, I applied these methodologies to various mass-mediated texts. I sent a query to the communications editors at Sage Publications, and, if I recall correctly, they asked to see the manuscript. They rejected it. I mentioned this rejection to Aaron one day when my wife and I were dining at his house. "I have this book on methods of analyzing media and popular culture," I said, "and I think it's really a good idea."

"Give me the book manuscript," he replied, "and I'll send it to someone who might be interested." I gave him a copy of the manuscript and he sent it off. Three weeks later I received a contract. It was from Sage Publications. Aaron had sent my manuscript to a different editor at Sage, one who liked it and had some helpful suggestions about how to modify it. The book was published in 1982 as *Media Analysis Techniques*. This textbook is still going strong—now in its third edition. As one of the editors of the book told me, "It took off like a rocket!" This story is to exemplify that you never can tell what will happen with a book once you write it. Do not give up hope and do not get discouraged when an editor rejects your book. I'll say it again: Do not take editorial rejections personally. Likewise, do not take negative reviews of your books personally. If I had become depressed after rejection, I probably would have stopped writing after my first book.

The Production Process

Getting a book accepted is only the first step to getting it published. Once a publisher accepts your book, you will be dealing with several different kinds of editors. The responsibilities of each of these editors is described in the chart below.

Kinds of Editors

Acquisition Editors: They find books to publish.
Development Editors: They help writers focus on important subjects.
Production Editors: They coordinate the design and production of the book.
Art Editors: They deal with visual aspects of the book.
Copyeditors: They check over the manuscript for errors.

Let's suppose you have written a book that, after a series of peer reviews and revisions, has been accepted by a publisher's acquisition editor and its editorial committee and is about to enter the production process. Your editor might have some suggestions about parts of the book to be developed and new topics to include. Once you've satisfied your editors, and your editor has been able to convince the company's editorial committee to accept your book, this is what *usually* happens.

You will receive an author's questionnaire from the publisher's marketing department, asking you questions that involve how the book might be marketed, what is special about it, which books it will compete with, who might be willing to write promotional blurbs for it, and other issues relevant to marketing the book. Often this will come to you around the same time you receive the book contract.

Your manuscript may be given to a development editor, who will have suggestions about your manuscript such as new topics to consider, organization of the chapters in your book, and additional graphs and tables you should consider including in the book. Once you've satisfied your acquisition editor and a development editor (if you've been asked to work with one), your book is

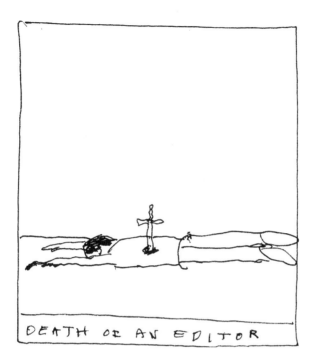

DEATH OF AN EDITOR

ready to move into the production process. Not all publishers have development editors—you'll mostly find them in the introductory textbook and trade book world where larger expected sales can justify paying for additional editorial work. For more scholarly presses, the acquisition editors serve this function.

Your finished manuscript will be given to a production editor. Your production editor will be responsible for designing the book or coordinating with a designer—determining what size the book will be, how many pages it will have, what typefaces will be used, and how large the margins will be. The production editor often works with an art editor, who handles the images in the book and other aesthetic considerations; a designer might handle the art as well. Someone will be found to create the cover. It may be a freelance cover designer or the publisher may have an in-house artist or art director for this task.

Your production editor will try to make certain that you have permission forms (if your acquisition editor has not already done so) for all quotations from books that don't fall under fair use—usually a quotation of more than three hundred words, or the use of any charts, graphs, or photographs from sources that are not in the public domain. There is a controversy about how many words can be used, under fair use, without permission from a publisher, and different rules apply for journal articles, poetry, and song lyrics. You should check with your editor if you have any questions about whether you need to obtain permission to reprint material. Some publishers have standard permission forms. Below I offer a sample permission form, one that I actually used, that you can adapt for your own purposes.

Arthur Asa Berger, Ph.D.
Broadcast & Electronic Communication Arts Department
San Francisco State University
San Francisco, CA 94l32
TEL (415) 3381788 FAX (415) 338-1168

Date:

To: Permissions Department
Rowman & Littlefield
4501 Forbes Blvd. Suite 200
Lanham, MD

In a forthcoming book, *Thailand Tourism,* to be published by Haworth Hospitality Press, 2007, I would like to include the following:

"Everyday Life and the Exotic" chart from *Deconstructing Travel*

Peirce's Trichotomy Chart from *Media and Society*

This material will be used in a book, tentatively titled *Thailand Tourism,* by Arthur Asa Berger. Tentative price: $24.95. Proposed publication date: 2007.

May we have permission to reprint your above-referenced material in our book, and in future revisions thereof, published by Haworth or its licensees, including nonexclusive world rights? Should you not control the rights in their entirety, would you tell me to whom I should write? Proper acknowledgment of title, artist or creative source, and publisher will be given. If this is agreeable, please sign and return this release at your earliest convenience. Thank you for your kind consideration.

Sincerely yours,

Arthur Asa Berger

Permission is granted to the request as outlined above:

Name:

Position:

Date:

The production editor will send your manuscript to a copyeditor. Usually copyeditors are freelancers, although some publishers have in-house copyeditors. In the good old days, copyeditors worked on hard copy and sent back manuscripts with many pages full of Post-It notes with comments and suggestions. Nowadays most copyeditors work on the electronic files of the book and use a word-processing feature (usually called "track changes") that indicates changes they wish to make in a colored typeface. Your comments, answers to their author queries, and replies to their changes, are shown in a different color.

Copyeditors polish your writing, fix spelling errors, and make sure that you haven't made any mistakes in your manuscript, like spelling a given author's name two different ways, or forgetting to indicate what page a passage you quoted comes from or not including a source in the bibliography. Copyeditors have saved my neck a number of times, and you'll be amazed at how clever they are and how picky they can be. On rare occasions, they want to make changes that will affect the meaning of what you've written, so be careful when reviewing the copyediting. You, as the author, have the final word, of course. I've learned over the years to be very grateful to my copyeditors. They approach your manuscript with a fresh mind, which helps explain why they can see problems in your manuscript that you couldn't.

When you've finished reviewing the copyedited manuscript, you return it to the copyeditor, who looks at what you've done and may have additional questions for you. Note that the copyedited manuscript is your last chance to do any fiddling with your verbiage. As the production process progresses, changes become more and more expensive to make and the publisher becomes less and less agreeable to making them.

Once the copyeditor is satisfied that the manuscript is in proper shape, it is generally sent back to your production editor, who will confirm the changes made and send it to typesetters, who prepare page proofs of your book. Your task in reading the page proofs is to make sure the typesetters haven't left out material or introduced new errors. Aside from correcting a misspelled word or rectifying any typesetting errors, your changes are expected to be minimal. Publishers usually hire a professional to proofread your pages at the same time.

Making an Index

Most publishers require an index for your book. Either a professional indexer can compile the index for you—and it is very costly to use their services—or you can prepare the index yourself. You can purchase inexpensive indexing software that makes indexing a relatively easy task. Before I had an indexing program, I used stacks of three- by five-inch cards. With each index entry, I had to find the proper card in the stack or create a new one. I decided to purchase an inexpensive indexing program, INDEXX, twenty years ago, and it has saved me thousands of dollars in indexing fees over the years. The program requires me to type in names and subjects, and then it organizes this material alphabetically.

You send the completed index to your production editor. Once the index has been reviewed, it will be typeset and the book will be printed. While each of these steps takes only a few weeks, the queue can be long at a busy publishing house. The entire process from submission of the final manuscript to receiving a printed copy of the book can be as short as three or four months or as long as two years. Because the publisher is investing in the production of the book, they decide the speed of the schedule, determine which editors you will work with, and have the final say in the design and manufacture of the book.

Print-on-Demand Publishing

I once read somewhere that the oldest example of printing found contained the statement, "Children no longer obey their parents and everyone is writing books." The authenticity of that statement is dubious, but the thoughts expressed are apropos. While everyone, or seemingly everyone, is writing books, most certainly aren't publishing them—at least not with conventional publishers.

Thanks to print-on-demand, Internet publishing ventures, such as iUniverse and Xlibris (both of which charge a few hundred dollars for the cheapest publishing of a book) and www.Lulu.com (which typesets a book for free and only charges you for the copies you print), it is much easier to print your own book. You can upload the file for a book you've written, have these companies automatically format it, and "publish" it yourself. At the current average rates, you'll pay nine or ten dollars for each copy of your book. The problem with these publishers is that they don't attempt to sell the book or improve your writing. If you want to use those services, you will be charged extra. So if you opt for the self-publishing route, you are unlikely to sell many copies of your book. Self-published books, I should add, usually aren't accepted as publications by university hiring, tenure, and promotion committees.

If you can use your book as a text in your courses, that's a different matter. For example, you can publish a textbook with Lulu for ten to fifteen dollars, depending upon how many pages the book is and how much you give yourself for a royalty. If you then use the book in your courses, it allows you to see how well it works and which sections need rewriting, at the same time providing your students with an inexpensive textbook. In the end, you will have a finished and tested book to send to any publishers you successfully query.

As you can see, publishing a book is complex and involves a great deal of work. Academics rarely invest a fraction of the research on publishing as they do on the project itself. But the effort is worth it because, after your book has been published, you can be confident that you've made a contribution to knowledge. If your book finds an audience, you will experience another reward—a royalty statement and check every six or twelve months.

Notes on Other Writing Genres

Philosophies, histories, literary essays, theories of economics, studies in government and law, the finds of sociology, the investigations of science—all these, however different, have for their purpose to explain. Although exposition often is formal and academic, it appears also in magazines and newspapers, in any place where people look for explanations. It is the most common kind of writing, the sort with which we conduct our workday affairs—the business letter, the doctor's case study, the lawyer's brief, the engineer's report—and the writing with which we attempt to control our world, whether our means of doing so is a complicated system of philosophy or a cookbook.

—Thomas S. Kane and Leonard J. Peters,
Writing Prose: Techniques and Purposes, 169

A Society of Transmitters
I live in a society of *transmitters* (being one myself): each person I meet or who writes to me, sends me a book, a text, an outline, a prospectus, a protest, an invitation to a performance, an exhibition, etc. The pleasure of writing, of producing, makes itself felt on all sides; but the circuit being commercial, free production remains clogged, hysterical, and somehow bewildered; most of the time, the texts and the performances proceed where there is no demand for them; they encounter, unfortunately for them, "relations" and not friends, still less partners; so that this kind of collective ejaculation of writing, in which one might see the *utopian* scene of a free society (in which pleasure would circulate without the intermediary of money), reverts today to the apocalypse.

—Roland Barthes, *Roland Barthes,* 81

Most of the daily writing we do, as Kane and Peters point out in the quotation on the previous page, is exposition and involves many "minor" or everyday genres, such as writing e-mails and sending faxes. The most important writing we do as academics, as I suggested earlier, involves writing our dissertations, reports, proposals, articles for scholarly publications, and books, such as scholarly studies or textbooks. In this chapter, I touch briefly on other writing genres and the means of delivering them that will be useful to you in your academic career. If you want in-depth examinations of a specific writing genre, consult the further resources section in this book.

I will begin with e-mail (electronic mail), then discuss sending faxes, preparing conference papers and presentations—both written ones and those using PowerPoint. Finally, I will offer important insights into planning and writing theses and dissertations.

A Primer on E-mailed Messages

Electronic mail (e-mail or email) is, technically speaking, a medium we use to send various kinds of messages—informal letters, notes, copies of articles we've read, images, manuscripts for articles and books, and so on. E-mailed messages are more informal than letters. This is, in part, because e-mail responses are more immediate; we receive and respond to them quickly, and in our haste to dash them off, we often compose them in a casual—sometimes careless—manner.

What we must keep in mind, however, is that though e-mailed messages are personal and informal in nature, they are *public* documents. The person who receives your e-mailed message can forward it to others—or may even post it on the web and make it accessible to a large number of people. If you send an e-mail from your university or to someone in a university, it can be held on the school's server and retrieved by members of the administration or others if they have a desire to do so.

Always include a brief but descriptive subject line. Having an informative subject line helps the recipients of your message learn what your message is about. It also helps you, if you are expecting a reply, to quickly determine the subject of the reply without having to read the body of the e-mail. A person I once worked with used "Question" for every subject line of every e-mail. This created difficulties for me in filing, prioritizing, and searching messages received from him.

Cautionary Notes about E-mailed Messages

Think twice about sending copies of your e-mails and articles of interest that you've found to others. Some people receive so many e-mails regularly that they spend an enormous amount of time going through their e-mail messages. I have two e-mail addresses—one for friends, editors, and others with whom I'm in frequent contact and another for everyone else—to isolate advertisements sent by e-mail and to reduce electronic spam. Most of the proposals I get from Nigeria go to the second address, but everyone is bothered by spam and it's impossible to avoid completely. You can minimize your exposure to spam by carefully guarding your e-mail address and not sharing it with those you don't know.

As with memos, be extremely careful about what you write in e-mail messages. Once you press the send button, you've lost control of the message. Never write an e-mail when you are angry or upset; you will probably regret having sent that e-mail at a later date. Before replying to an e-mail that has made you angry or upset, give yourself about a day or two to cool down. Always review your e-mail messages for spelling and writing errors, for typos, and for other mistakes.

Think about what information to include in your signature block, the material that comes under your name in your e-mail messages. You might want to include your title, position, university, snail-mail address, phone number, e-mail address, and fax number, to make it easier for others to get in touch with you by means other than e-mail. Having your e-mail address on your signature means people can send an e-mail to you just by clicking on the address without having to scroll to the top of the message and hit reply.

E-mail is handy for communicating with editors and sending copies of articles you've written or even sending book manuscripts to editors.

After I've sent query letters to editors, I send e-mail messages with copies of my manuscripts if they are interested in the article or book I described in my query. I also send queries to editors I haven't worked with about ideas I have for articles and books. Now most copyeditors send the copyedited version of articles and books—and in some cases page proofs—to authors in attachments to e-mails.

I will conclude this discussion of e-mail messages by offering some suggestions:

- Never send angry or insulting e-mails to anyone.
- Keep e-mail messages as short as possible.
- Put the subject of your message in the subject line.
- Start with a salutation of some kind, not the body of message.
- Don't give your e-mail address to everyone.
- Avoid sexist language.
- Don't open an attachment unless you're certain it is virus-free. Certainly don't send one that you suspect has a virus.

- Advise recipients of messages when it is acceptable to use "reply all." Check carefully before hitting "send."
- Find out if your recipient's program can accept large attachments.
- If replying to a message that asks questions, indicate which questions you are answering.
- Write economically but not tersely or in an abrupt manner.
- Indicate deadlines for replies when applicable.
- When replying to long messages, delete the original message from your reply to avoid clutter.
- Don't spam people with jokes, advertisements, or other material that may upset them.
- If you have a number of questions to ask, put them all in one e-mail message.

Electronic mail is the workhorse of electronic communication. According to one site on Google, worldwide we send 31 billion e-mail messages per day. Another site says we send 171 billion e-mail messages each day. As useful and ubiquitous as e-mail messages are, sometimes it is better to send faxes, the subject of my next section.

Faxes

Faxes (short for facsimile transmissions) are useful when we want to send a copy of something that has already been printed or has been written, annotated, or created by hand. We can, of course, scan a document into our computer and send it as an attachment to an e-mail message, but it is often easier to send the document as a fax. Faxes are useful for sending forms that cannot be filled out on the Internet and documents that have charts, graphs, and other graphic material. The speed of your fax machine, the number of pages being faxed, and the complexity of the graphic material to be sent will affect the speed of the fax transmittal. And unlike e-mail, which doesn't have a "per message" fee, faxes use telephone lines and cost money to send.

Faxes usually come with a cover form, indicating who sent the fax and who is receiving it, along with other information. You can download templates for cover forms from the Internet. They usually include some variation of the following:

- To (name of receiver):
- Fax number of receiver:
- From (name of sender):
- Fax number of sender:
- Phone number of sender:

- Date of fax:
- Subject line
- Number of pages in the fax (in addition to cover sheet)
- Comments about the fax

Faxes can now be sent using your computer and the Internet, so fax machines are no longer necessary and faxes can be seen, without stretching logic too far, as a variant of the traditional e-mail message. The same cautions that apply to e-mail messages therefore apply to faxes.

Often a university department has only one fax machine, so realize that even if you mark the cover form to your fax as "personal" or "private," that fax may be seen and read, sometimes accidentally, by a number of people. So be careful about what information you include in the faxes you send to others. It also isn't considered good etiquette to send long faxes, unless you've checked with the recipient first.

Conference Papers

One important thing to remember about conference papers is that generally you are limited to around twenty minutes for your presentation. Since it takes about three minutes to read one page of double-spaced material, this means limit your paper to around six pages.

If you spend more than your allotted time, you decrease the time available for other speakers. I once was the third speaker on a panel at a conference. The first speaker finished in twenty minutes, but the second speaker, the one before me—despite numerous attempts by the moderator to get him to stop—took thirty-five minutes for his presentation, which left me with only five minutes for mine.

Rehearse your presentation a few times to prepare for how long it takes you to finish. If you find you are going over your time limit, delete or skip over some portions of your presentation. Some presenters read every word in their papers, which most others find quite tedious, especially since many presenters provide copies of their papers for those attending the sessions or make them available on the Internet. It is better to provide the gist of your argument, reading only small portions of the paper here and there, unless the topic is complicated and demands that every word be read.

Since a conference paper is rather short, carefully limit its scope and choose a subject that can be covered adequately in five or six pages or around twenty minutes. When you submit an abstract of your proposal to conference committees, explain why your paper should be accepted—that is, point out what your presentation adds to the subject and what new insights it offers to the academic field. Presentation papers must take shortcuts and get to the meat of the subject as quickly as possible.

Many speakers now use PowerPoint for their presentations. But even with PowerPoint, speakers often include too much text on each slide, which they then read to the audience. This is not optimal for a presentation. PowerPoint is useful for generating images, charts, diagrams, graphs, and other visual phenomena. But you are not using it to your best advantage when you generate long passages of text.

Theses and Dissertations

There are a number of books available about writing theses (for a master's degree) and dissertations (for a doctorate). (See further resources for a few.) In the earlier chapters, I addressed many of the topics that writers face, regardless of what kind of a work they are writing, and these chapters will help you to write your theses and dissertations. In addition, here are three very important hints:

1. Narrow your focus!
2. Then, narrow your focus again!
3. Then, narrow your narrowed focus again!

The problem most graduate students have is they want to tackle large subjects.

When I was working on my doctorate many years ago, a friend of mine in the American Studies Program at the University of Minnesota decided he would write his dissertation on "The Failure of the West." Eventually, this proved too large to take on, and he ended up writing about a minor regional American writer instead. Likewise, I went in to see my graduate advisor with the grand notion of doing a comprehensive study of utopian thought—and came out instead with an analysis of social and political themes in the comic strip *Li'l Abner*. "You wrote a very good paper on *Li'l Abner* in the course on American political thought. Why not expand it?" he said. I took his advice.

There was another student in the American Studies Program who wrote a dissertation that was more than seven hundred pages. "One of my thesis advisors wanted more on this subject," she told me, "and another one wanted more on that subject, and before I knew it I had written seven hundred pages." That meant that five very busy professors on her committee had to read (or were supposed to read) those seven hundred pages of her dissertation. After that experience, the program passed a rule limiting the length of dissertations to two hundred pages. The moral of this disquisition: narrow your focus and find a topic that is manageable and can be done in a reasonable amount of time.

The Writer's Life

Years ago, at a party full of writers and would-be writers given by a literary agent, a young woman approached me and asked, "Are you literary?"

"Yes," I replied.

She smiled. "Have you published?" she asked.

"Yes, I have," I said.

"How nice," she replied. "Are your books fiction or nonfiction?"

"I write nonfiction books," I answered, "but most people think they're fiction."

The tools and genres that I've discussed in this book are primarily related to nonfiction, but my suggestions can be adapted for most other genres in print or electronic media.

In the next section I offer a Coda, with some final thoughts on writing as a means of personal validation, as a way of discovering things hidden in your unconscious, and as what Roland Barthes described as "the pleasure of the text."

Coda

In composition studies, [Ken] Bruffee, Patricia Bizzell, and others have questioned traditional notions about the autonomy of the author and traditional assumptions that writing and reading, in Bruffee's words, are "intrinsically individual, asocial activities." They use the idea that writing takes place in social contexts to argue that the production of meaning in written language itself is a social or collaborative process. What goes through a writer's mind during composing—what the Soviet psychologist Lev Vygotsky (1962) calls "inner speech"—is not the preparation of private and individual thought for public presentation. Rather, Bruffee argues, the writer's consciousness is constituted by public and social talk internalized, by conversation taking place within. In this view, the author is no longer the nineteenth-century individualist but rather a social function in a larger system of dependencies. Writing is not so much the personal expression (and property) of the individual author. Instead, Bruffee says, if "thought is internalized conversation, then writing is internalized conversation re-externalized."

—Peter Elbow, "In Defense of Private Writing," 141

Often, when people first sit down to write, they begin a sentence and immediately take a dislike to the way it is worded and start again. This is the editor interfering with the writer. Both are essential, but both should be kept in their places. The writer writes, the editor edits. The writer writes without worrying about what the niggly editorial commentary is saying—"Oh, what would so and so say about that?" or "I don't think that is the proper way to say it," or "Is that the correct academic style?" The writer just writes without stopping, to rethink, to correct, to stand back and pass judgment. Simply write on your subject.

—Christine S. Smedley, Mitchell Allen, and associates,
Getting Your Book Published, 29

Writing is *always* hard work. A writer needs to find ideas to write about and time to revise and rewrite. But like riding a bicycle, driving a car, dancing, cooking a meal, and countless other activities, writing gets easier the more often you do it. After a while, you learn to internalize certain behaviors that previously took a lot of conscious thought and effort. You may find that writing in your journal helps you develop ideas and think about new writing projects. You may discover that some of the suggestions offered in this book—about organizing your time, outlining, revising what you've written on hard copy, and other aspects of writing—start becoming second nature. And when you've published your first article or first book, you'll probably feel a sense of accomplishment that will spur you on to other literary projects.

Publishing as a Form of Personal Validation

Writers are, in most cases, searching for two things: first, an editor who likes what they write, second, an audience. But without an approving editor, one who can convince an editorial board that a book or article is worth publishing, authors can't hope to find an audience, except through blogging or self-publishing. There is an element of adventure to writing, because you never know how your work will be received or what its fate will be.

When a publisher accepts your book, it's always a thrill. That's because getting your work accepted by a traditional publisher, who pays for producing and marketing the book, is validation of your ideas and your writing. Publishers are gatekeepers, and one has let you pass through the gate. Once published, your book may not get many adoptions and may sink into the mire, or it may do tolerably well and provide some decent royalties, or it may take off and do very well. You just never know. In my books, I always include my e-mail address in the about the author section, which is usually found at the back of a book. That way, readers can get in touch with me—either to tell me how much they liked the book or to complain about errors they believe I've made. I don't receive many e-mail messages from readers, but I've gotten enough to give me an idea of how the works have been received. Sometimes you may even receive nice messages about your book from readers who tell you how valuable the book has been to them.

There are, then, many gratifications and rewards—not always monetary—involved in writing. I'll be discussing more of these throughout this chapter. These gratifications compensate for all of the rejections from editors and the nasty comments you sometimes get from the anonymous professors who reviewed your manuscript while it was being considered for publication. Of course, some professors are positive about the manuscripts and offer useful suggestions, so it isn't always a painful process. No matter what, keep writing and do not let rejections, negative reviews, or anything else get you down.

Writing as an Act of Discovery

One reason I love to write is that, in the process of researching and writing, I discover things of interest and use to me. As I write, certain matters buried in the unconscious parts of my psyche somehow come to light, and I discover relationships between things I had never seen before. Much of this takes place as I write in my journals and play around with ideas. This act of discovery is exciting. When I write, I honestly can say that I never can be sure what I'm going to write about, and I'm always curious to find out.

When I wrote *Bloom's Morning*, I devoted several pages in one of my journals to brainstorming on the topics I would be covering in the book: king-sized beds, broadloom carpets, pajamas, toasters, electric shavers, and so on. I listed aspects of interest for each of these topics, and yet when I started writing the book, additional and different ideas about each of these topics came to me from "out of the blue," so to speak. That is, I knew I wanted to write about the "secret significance" or "hidden meaning" of each of these topics, but I wasn't sure what conclusions I would reach. As I wrote, I started figuring out what I would write about them through a process I find hard to explain. New insights and discoveries popped into my head as I wrote. As an example, I offer a passage about the symbolic significance of stockings:

> If the foot has an erotic component to it and in fact often functions like a phallus, then stockings have a significance that becomes quite obvious. If their function is to mediate, to protect the foot, and to contain body excretions, is it not possible to see putting on a stocking as being similar to putting on a condom? . . . And the fact that our feet smell and are subject to fungus infections such as athlete's foot suggests the kind of anxiety and ambivalence many men feel about sex. Woman's genitals also smell (so we've learned from advertising), and we can get infections or even die (due to AIDS) from sexual activity. Thus our problems with our feet trigger in our psyches various ambiguous feelings and anxieties we have about sexuality.

Some will see this passage as "far-fetched," but I've always felt it is better to follow ideas where they lead and find interesting relationships rather than worry about whether some people will find your notions ridiculous.

As we've seen, keeping a journal is useful because you can practice writing and, to use a sports metaphor, warm up for other writing you might want to do. There's no question in my mind that my style of writing evolved (as my handwriting deteriorated) over the course of writing more than eighty-five journals.

The Pleasure of the Text

I've never had writer's block. I love to write, and I get a great deal of pleasure from the process of writing—thinking up books to write and continually rewriting them. Writing is a creative activity and is, like all creative activities, wonderfully gratifying and fulfilling, despite being hard work.

The French critic Roland Barthes wrote *The Pleasure of the Text,* which considers the other side of the creative process: the pleasure—or the "erotics"— of reading. But one cannot address reading without considering writing, so Barthes has much to say about writing as well. Barthes was a superb stylist who created many clever neologisms and wrote in a very sensuous and often elliptical manner. *The Pleasure of the Text* is a collection of short passages about words connected to reading, arranged in alphabetical order—from Affirmation to Voice.

In the passage that follows, Barthes writes about the relationship that exists between writers and readers:

> If I read this sentence, this story, or this word with pleasure, it is because they were written in pleasure (such pleasure does not contradict the writer's complaints). But the opposite? Does writing in pleasure guarantee—guarantee me, the writer—my readers' pleasure? Not at all. I must seek out this reader (must "cruise" him) *without knowing where he is.* A site of bliss is then created. It is not the reader's "person" that is necessary to me, it is this site: the possibility of a dialectics of desire, of an *unpredictability* of bliss: the bets are not placed, there can still be a game. (4)

What Barthes is discussing in this passage involves the dilemma all writers face. Whenever we write, we have an audience in mind, but we cannot know whether we will reach this audience and how the audience will react to what we have written. So writing has an element of unpredictability about it. Writers, Barthes would say, are always playing a game and can be never sure how it will turn out.

Barthes calls our attention to the imaginary bond between writers and those for whom they write. If you write with pleasure, he says, you cannot be sure that your readers will experience that pleasure when they read what you have written. I addressed this earlier—finding an audience that will take pleasure in your work is a challenge that all writers must face. But even if you can't guarantee that your readers will find pleasure in your writing, you can hope that they will. Writers can't be sure about a potential reader's pleasure or acceptance.

I hope, for example, that you found this book useful and a pleasure to read, but I can't be sure how you'll react to it. You might not like my sense of humor or my informal style of writing; you might feel that a book on writing should be serious, formal, and impersonal. I try to write in a manner that is both entertaining and instructive and always fear that some of my readers will feel that I've done neither.

Writing as Conversation

In chapter 4, I offered a discussion of Labov's work on the structure of conversations and suggested that we think about writing as a conversation authors have with their readers. Let me now add some insights from Russian literary theorist M. M. Bakhtin. Bakhtin explains that speech is dialogic—and so, I would add, is writing. What Bakhtin wrote about conversation also applies to written forms of communication. As he explains in his essay "Discourse on the Novel," in *The Dialogic Imagination*:

> The word in living conversation is directly, blatantly, oriented toward a future answer-word: it provokes an answer, anticipates it and structures itself in the answer's direction. Forming itself in an atmosphere of the already spoken, the word is at the same time determined by that which has not yet been said but which is needed and anticipated by the answering word. Such is the situation in any living dialogue. (280)

Writing is, in some ways, like having a conversation with your reader, who becomes an imagined listener. The words we write are connected to those we already have written and to those we anticipate writing.

The critic David Lodge makes the same point in *The Modes of Modern Writing*:

> One quality we expect of all writing is continuity. Writing is a one-sided conversation. As every student, and every critic, knows, the most difficult aspect of composing an essay or thesis or book is to put one's scattered thoughts into an ideal order which will appear to have a seamless logical inevitability in its progress from one topic to another without distorting or omitting any important point. This book itself contains innumerable sentences and phrases included not primarily to convey information but to construct smooth links between one topic and another. . . . And it is by its continuity that a discursive text persuades

the reader, implying that no other ordering of its data could be intellectually as satisfying. (231)

When we write, Lodge suggests, much of the work we do doesn't involve conveying information but entails providing links between ideas. It is through our transitions and other rhetorical techniques that we inform and persuade our readers. If writing is like a conversation, we must be certain that we provide all the details and necessary links between ideas that make our conversations intelligible and interesting. One implication of Lodge's statement is that when we write, we must pay particular attention to planning the texts before we start writing them, since the structure is so important. We also must consider the connective tissue that holds the body of our writing together to be of the utmost importance. I have covered these matters in my discussions of transitions, the importance of logical structure, and the use of other techniques to achieve your objectives. The process of writing involves choosing words, one after another, from an almost infinite number of possibilities, to put down on paper. Yet, as Bakhtin explains, once you've written a word, certain other words are logically and implicitly called for, just as in conversation.

I take leave of you here, ending this conversation for now, hoping that you've found my book worth reading. I also hope that it helps you learn to write in a more accessible and more readable manner. I've offered my own strategies as well as technical information about the formal structure of different kinds of academic texts. It's one thing to learn the theory—to learn the steps of the dance, so to speak. The hard part is actually dancing—that is, using what you've learned about writing in the texts you write. You may not end up a Fred Astaire, but you might very well cut a fine figure on the dance floor.

I'd be interested in your comments about this book and any suggestions you may have to offer. You can get in touch with me by e-mail at arthurasaberger@yahoo.com. Good luck, and may you have many PIP (pages in print) in the course of your academic career.

Further Resources

There are books about every aspect of writing, from those about writing in general to books that address grammar, research, documentation, and special kinds of writing such as writing articles for journals and writing memos, letters, and proposals. I've listed a number of these that you might want to consult as you pursue your interest in writing. Some of these works are classics, written years ago; some are updated versions of previously published books; others were published in recent years.

General Writing

Kane, Thomas S., and Leonard J. Peters. 1986. *Writing Prose: Techniques and Purposes.* New York: Oxford University Press.

Ross-Larson, Bruce. 2002. *Writing for the Information Age.* New York: Norton.

Silvia, Paul J. 2007. *How to Write a Lot: A Practical Guide to Productive Academic Writing.* Washington, D.C.: American Psychological Association.

Zinsser, William K. 2006. *On Writing Well: The Classic Guide to Writing Nonfiction, 30th Anniversary Edition.* New York: Harper-Collins.

Grammar

Hale, Constance. 1999. *Sin and Syntax: How to Craft Wickedly Effective Prose.* New York: Broadway Books.

Hale, Contance, and Jessie Scanlon. 1999. *Wired Style: Principles of English Usage in the Digital Age.* New York: Broadway Books.

Strumpf, Michael, and Auriel Douglas. 2004. *The Grammar Bible: Everything You Wanted to Know about Grammar but Didn't Know Whom to Ask.* New York: Owl Books.

Strunk, William Jr., and E. B. White. 1999. *The Elements of Style, Fourth Edition.* New York: Longman.

Research

Barzun, Jacques, and Henry F. Graff. 1957. *The Modern Researcher.* New York: Harcourt, Brace & World.

Documentation Style

American Psychological Association. 2001. *Publication Manual of the American Psychological Association, Fifth Edition.* Washington, D.C.: American Psychological Association.

Gibaldi, Joseph. 2003. *MLA Handbook for Writers of Research Papers, Sixth Edition.* New York: Modern Language Association.

Lipson, Charles. 2006. *Cite Right: A Quick Guide to Citation Styles—MLA, APA, Chicago, the Sciences, Professions, and More.* Chicago Guides to Writing, Editing and Publishing. Chicago: University of Chicago Press.

University of Chicago Press. 2003. *The Chicago Manual of Style: The Essential Guide for Writers, Editors, and Publishers, Fifteenth Edition.* Chicago: University of Chicago Press.

Writing Articles and Books

Brewer, Robert Lee, and Chuck Sambuchino, eds. 2007. *Writer's Market 2008.* Cincinnati, OH: Writer's Digest Books.

Germano, William. 2001. *Getting It Published: A Guide for Scholars and Anyone Else Serious about Serious Books.* Chicago: University of Chicago Press.

———. 2005. *From Dissertation to Book.* Chicago: University of Chicago Press.

Glatthorn, Allan A.. 2002. *Publish or Perish—The Educator's Imperative: Strategies for Writing Effectively for Your Profession and Your School.* Thousand Oaks, CA: Corwin Press.

Kirsch, Jonathan. 2007. *Kirsch's Handbook of Publishing Law: For Authors, Publishers, Editors and Agents, Second Edition.* Los Angeles: Silman-James Press.

Luey, Beth, ed. 2007. *Revising Your Dissertation: Advice from Leading Editors.* Berkeley: University of California Press.

Barry Wellman. How to Write—and Edit—a Paper. Accessed at www.chass.utoronto.ca/~wellman/publications/writing/writing.pdf.

———. Writing for International Refereed Journals. Accessed at http://home.iscte.pt/~apad/risco01/textos/Barry-Wellman-Writing-for-International-Refereed-Journals.doc.

E-mail

Cavanagh, Christina. 2003. *Managing Your E-mail: Thinking Outside the Inbox.* Hoboken, NJ: Wiley.

Fisher Chan, Janis. 2005. *E-mail: A Write It Well Guide—How to Write and Manage E-mail in the Workplace.* Oakland, CA: Write It Well.

Shipley, David, and Will Schwalbe. 2007. *Send: The Essential Guide to Email for Office and Home.* New York: Knopf.

Dissertations/Theses

Foss, Sonja K., and William Waters. 2007. *Destination Dissertation: A Traveler's Guide to a Done Dissertation.* Lanham, Md.: Rowman & Littlefield Publishers.

Race, Phil, and Brian Allison. 2007. *The Student's Guide to Preparing Dissertations and Theses.* London: RoutledgeFarmer.

Thomas, R. Murray, and Dale L. Brubaker. 2007. *Theses and Dissertations: A Guide to Planning, Research, and Writing.* Westport, CT: Bergin & Garvey.

Turabian, Kate L., Wayne Booth, Gregory C. Columb, and Joseph M. Williams. 2007. *A Manual for Writers of Research Papers, Theses, and Dissertations, Seventh Edition.* Chicago: University of Chicago Press.

Webster, William G. 1998. *21 Models for Developing and Writing Theses, Dissertations and Projects.* San Ramon, CA: Academic Scholarwrite.

Zerubavel, Eviatar. 1999. *The Clockwork Muse: A Practical Guide to Writing Theses, Dissertations, and Books.* Cambridge: MA: Harvard University Press.

Bibliography

Allen, Woody. 1976. "Selections from the Allen Notebooks." *Without Feathers*. New York: Warner Books.

———. 1978. "Spring Bulletin." *Getting Even*. Vintage

Aristotle. 1941. *The Basic Works of Aristotle*. Richard McKeon, ed. New York: Random House.

Bakhtin, M. M. 1981. *The Dialogic Imagination: Four Essays by M. M. Bakhtin*. M. Holquist, ed., C. Emerson, and M. Holquist, trans. Austin: University of Texas Press.

Barthes, Roland. 1975. *The Pleasure of the Text.*. New York: Hill and Wang.

———. 1977. *Roland Barthes*. Richard Howard, trans. New York: Hill and Wang.

Barzun, Jacques, and Henry R. Graff. 1970. *The Modern Researcher, Revised Edition*. New York: Harcourt, Brace & World.

Berger, Arthur Asa. 1993. *Improving Writing Skills: Memos, Letters, Reports, and Proposals*. Newbury Park, CA: Sage.

———. 1996. *Master of Demystification* 65 (February 25): 144.

———. 1997. *Bloom's Morning: Coffee, Comforters, and the Secret Meaning of Everyday Life*. Boulder, CO: Westview Press.

———. 1997. *Postmortem for a Postmodernist*. Walnut Creek, CA: AltaMira Press.

———. 2000. *Media and Communication Research Methods: An Introduction to Qualitative and Quantitative Approaches*. Thousand Oaks, CA: Sage Publications.

———. 2000. *The Hamlet Case*. Philadelphia: XLibris.

Blackwell Publishers. *Journal of Communication*. www.blackwell.com/joc. Accessed October 2007.

Blanshard, Brand. 1954. *On Philosophical Style*. Westport, CT: Greenwood.

Brogan, Kathryn S., ed. 2004. "Getting Published: Before Your First Sale," *2004: Writer's Market*. Cincinnati, OH: Writers Digest Books.

Buckley, Walter. 1967. *Sociology and Modern System Theory*. Upper Saddle River, NJ: Prentice-Hall.

de Saussure, Ferdinand. 1966 [1915]. *Course in General Linguistics*. Charles Bally and Albert Sechehaye, ed., Wade Baskin, trans. New York: McGraw-Hill.

Elbow, Peter. 1999. "In Defense of Writing: Consequences for Theory and Research." *Written Communication* 16(2) (April): 139–69.

Farb, Peter. 1974. *Word Play: What Happens When People Talk.* New York: Bantam Books.

Frank, Reuven. 1974. Quoted in E. J. Epstein, *News from Nowhere: Television and the News.* New York: Vintage.

Franklin, Benjamin. 1998. *Autobiography.* Mineola, NY: Dover.

Freud, Sigmund. 1897. Letter to Wilhelm Fleiss, October 15. Quoted in Martin Grotjahn, *Humor and the Subconscious.* New York: McGraw-Hill.

Gitlin, Todd. 1987. "Television Screens: Hegemony in Transition." *Media and Mass Culture.* David Lazare, ed. Berkeley: University of California Press.

———. 2001. *Media Unlimited.* New York: Henry Holt.

Hayakawa, S.I. 1978. *Language in Thought and Action, Fourth Edition.* New York: Harcourt Brace Jovanovich.

Hyers, Conrad. 1974. *Zen and the Comic Spirit.* Philadelphia: Westminster. .

Jakobson, Rowman. 1988. "Linguistics and Poetics." Quoted in David Lodge, ed., *Modern Criticism and Theory: A Reader.* New York: Longman.

Kaiser Family Foundation. 2007. "Food for Thought: Television Food Advertising to Children in the United States." Available at www.kff.org/entmedia/upload17618 .pdf. Accessed June 2007.

Kane, Thomas S., and Leonard J. Peters. 1986. *Writing Prose: Techniques and Purposes.* New York: Oxford University Press.

Kant, Immanuel. 1998. *Groundwork of the Metaphysics of Morals.* Cambridge: Cambridge University Press.

Lakoff, George, and Mark Johnson. 1980. *Metaphors We Live By.* Chicago: University of Chicago Press.

Lamott, Anne. 1995. *Bird by Bird: Some Instructions on Writing and Life.* New York: Anchor Books.

Layard, Austen H. J. 1853. *Discoveries in the Ruins of Nineveh and Babylon.* Quoted in J. Barzun and Henry F. Graff, *The Modern Researcher.* 1957. New York: Harbinger.

Lifton, Robert. 1970. "Who Is More Dry? Heroes of Japanese Youth." *History and Human Survival.* New York: Random House.

Lodge, David. 1977. *The Modes of Modern Writing: Metaphor, Metonymy, and the Typology of Modern Literature.* London: Arnold

McKercher, Bob, and Candace Fu. 2006. "Living on the Edge," *Annals of Tourism Research* 33(2).

Molière. *The Bourgeois Gentleman*, Act II, Scene 6.

Morris, Jan. 1982. "Delhi." *Destinations: Essays from Rolling Stone.* New York: Oxford University Press.

Nozick, Robert. *Philosophy 25: The Best Things in Life.* Harvard University Bulletin.

Orwell, George. 1946. "Politics and the English Language." *A Collection of Essays.* New York: Harvest Books.

Pirandello, Luigi. 1986. *Six Characters in Search of an Author.* London: Methuen.

Poria, Yaniv, and Yaniv Gvili. 2006. "Heritage Site Websites Content: The Need for Versatility." *Journal of Hospitality & Leisure Marketing: The International Forum for Research, Theory & Practice* 15(2).

Queneau, Raymond. 1981. *Exercises in Style.* New York: New Directions.

Richardson, Laurel. 1990. "Narrative and Sociology," *Journal of Contemporary Ethnology* 19:118.

Riessman, Catherine Kohler. 1993. *Narrative Analysis.* Newbury Park, CA: Sage Publications.

Smedley, Christine S., Mitchell Allen, and associates. 1993. *Getting Your Book Published.* Newbury Park, CA: Sage Publications

Stavans, Illan. 2007. "Wilson Critiqued Literature When Books Really Mattered." *San Francisco Chronicle,* December 9, M3.

Strunk, William Jr., and E. B. White. 1972. *The Elements of Style, Second Edition.* New York: Macmillan.

Swift, Jonathan. 1996 [1729]. "A Modest Proposal." *A Modest Proposal and Other Satirical Works.* Mineola, NY: Dover.

Thompson, Michael, Richard Ellis, and Aaron Wildavsky. 1990. *Cultural Theory.* Boulder, CO: Westview Press.

Trimble, John R.. 1975. *Writing with Style: Conversations on the Art of Writing.* Upper Saddle River, NJ: Prentice Hall.

Turabian, Kate L. 1967. *A Manual for Writers of Term Papers, Theses, and Dissertations.* Chicago: The University of Chicago Press.

Wellman, Barry. Writing for International Refereed Journals. Accessed at http://home.iscte.pt/~apad/risco01/textos/Barry-Wellman-Writing-for-International-Refereed-Journals.doc.

Wittgenstein, Ludwig. 1971 [1921]. "Understanding Depends on Tacit Conventions." *Tractatus Logico-Philosophicus.* London: Routledge & Regal Paul.

Zinnser, William. 1985. *On Writing Well: An Informal Guide to Writing Nonfiction, Revised and Enlarged Third Edition.* New York: Harper & Row.

Index

About the Author

Arthur Asa Berger is professor emeritus of Broadcast and Electronic Communication Arts at San Francisco State University, where he taught between 1965 and 2003. He graduated in 1954 from the University of Massachusetts, where he majored in literature and philosophy. He received an M.A. in journalism and creative writing from the University of Iowa in 1956. He was drafted shortly after graduating from Iowa and served in the U.S. Army in the Military District of Washington in Washington, D.C., where he was a feature writer and speech writer in the District's Public Information Office. He also wrote high school sports for the *Washington Post* on weekend evenings while in the army.

Berger spent a year touring Europe after he got out of the army and then attended the University of Minnesota, where he received a Ph.D. in American Studies in 1965. He wrote his dissertation on the comic strip *Li'l Abner*. From 1963 to 1964, he had a Fulbright scholarship in Italy and taught at the University of Milan. He spent a year as visiting professor at the Annenberg School for Communication at the University of Southern California in Los Angeles in 1984 and two months in the fall of 2007 as visiting professor at the School of Hotel and Tourism Management at the Hong Kong Polytechnic University.

Berger is the author of more than a hundred articles published in the United States and abroad, numerous book reviews, and more than sixty books on the mass media, popular culture, humor, tourism, and everyday life. Among his books are *Media Analysis Techniques* (third edition), *Media & Society* (second edition), *Seeing Is Believing: An Introduction to Visual Communication* (third edition), *Ads, Fads And Consumer Culture* (third edition), *The Art of Comedy Writing*, and *Shop 'Til You Drop: Consumer Behavior and American Culture.*

He has also written a number of comic academic mysteries such as *Postmortem for a Postmodernist, Mistake in Identity, The Mass Comm Murders: Five Media Theorists Self-Destruct,* and *Durkheim Is Dead: Sherlock Holmes Is Introduced to Sociological Theory.* His books have been translated into German, Italian, Russian, Arabic, Swedish, Korean, Turkish, and Chinese and he has lectured in more than a dozen countries in the course of his career.

Berger is married, has two children and three grandchildren, and lives in Mill Valley, California. He enjoys travel and dining in ethnic restaurants. He also occasionally lectures on cruise ships about media and popular culture. He can be reached by e-mail at arthurasaberger@yahoo.com.